Running From Crazy

By
Chrissie Anderson Peters

CAP Publishing
Bristol, TN

Running From Crazy

CAP Publishing
284 Midway Dr.
Bristol, TN 37620
www.ChrissieAndersonPeters.com, www.CAPWrites.com
Phone: 423.646.8659

This book is comprised of stories that are both fictional and nonfictional in nature, the nonfictional parts based on memories of the author. These memories may differ from the memories of others involved, but are set down as they are for the sake of art and telling specific stories. No malicious or falsified comments are intended by the author.

Book cover designed by Pat Shrader; book cover art copyright © 2013 Blue Ridge Expressions.

Printed in the United States of America

ISBN-13: 978-0-9852574-1-5
ISBN-10: 0985257415

Running From Crazy

By
Chrissie Anderson Peters

CAP Publishing

To those Friends of Mine who continue to stand by me through the craziness, or maybe even because of it.

To Russ, who knew about the craziness and said "I do," anyway. Thanks for never doubting and for always believing, even when I'm not so sure.

To Kacper, for asking when "our" book would be ready. I was beginning to think that it wouldn't ever be, but you made me realize once again that nothing I do is mine alone.

To J-Rhude (a.k.a., John Rhudy), and his Crew for talking me up in Tazewell when no one in my hometown seemed interested at all in my writing. You took a chance on me and I can't thank you enough.

To anyone else who has also tried to run, only to realize, in the end, that there are some things that cannot be left behind, but are an inherent part of who we are, no matter how hard we wish differently; *to those* who understand that it is in how we choose to deal with it that we separate ourselves from the craziness and find our true paths of what passes for sanity in this life.

Chrissie Anderson Peters

Advance Praise for *Running From Crazy*:

"*Running from Crazy* is a delightful collage of memories woven into prose and poetry that is at times poignant and heartrending and at others is humorous and down-right wacky. Chrissie [Anderson] Peters has the remarkable ability to step back from her life and write about those terribly human moments – the ones we wish had never happened – until we grow-up and realize they are the exact moments that make us the people we are today." -- Rebecca Elswick, author of *Mama's Shoes*

"In *Running From Crazy* Chrissie [Anderson] Peters collects essays, poems and stories focusing on life's eternal mysteries, such as how to forgive absent fathers, insensitive coaches, and cruel college football players. Part memoir, part family history, part homage to the mountains she loves, the book provides an interesting sampling of Peters' eclectic interests and talents." – Rita Sims Quillen, author of *Her Secret Dream* (poetry) and *Hiding Ezra* (forthcoming novel)

Preface

"Do you really think that people are going to want to read a book called *Running From Crazy?*" my mom asked me when I told her my proposed title.

"Lord, I hope so!" was my first thought. That was closely followed by, "*Well, why wouldn't they?*" Then I looked at her and assured her that I thought everyone would be intrigued by it. And that was several weeks before I realized that there was a documentary about the Hemingway family just released with the same title, even though that documentary was beginning to make the rounds in the world of film as I was starting to tie up my textual loose ends for this collection of stories, essays, and poems.

I am notoriously horrible with coming up with titles for my work, a bad thing for any writer. My last collection was saved from the fate of being named *So Far* only because my dear friend Denton Loving had the common decency to tell me how horrific that title really was, something that author Margaret Atwood told me when I met her and shared the story with her at the Book Festival in Edinburgh, Scotland, in August 2013, I should be thankful for every day! (And I am!)

With *Running From Crazy*, however, I had not just come up with a title; I had, for all intents and purposes, shared one of my innermost secrets, a lifelong adage, if you will, that always brought chuckles from those I said it to, but that also secretly shamed me and frightened me to my core. For I *have* been running from crazy my whole life! Mental illness has cursed members of my family for several generations. In more than one family line, there have been family members who were taken to the state mental hospital in Marion, Virginia. Some of them left there alive and some died there; but none of them ever left intact. Mental hospitals of the past were horrible places, not centers of rehabilitation and assistance. And one might be taken there for any of a number of reasons, many of which we might not even consider to be truly "mental" in nature today. Yet the stigma existed then that still remains: the crazy house, the loony bin.

I was actually born in Marion, that small town in Southwestern Virginia, where the state hospital is. I remember being teased in school about it when I told people. "No," I would shout at them! *Not in that hospital!* In Smyth County Community Hospital! *The other hospital in Marion!*"

From an early age, I was discouraged from talking to guidance counselors and other authority figures about "problems" or "family stuff." They weren't to be trusted. We should take those things to God; He would meet our needs. As a kid, and especially as an adolescent, I wasn't always convinced that God was listening to me, especially with so many other things going on in the world. But I learned that a lot of guidance counselors and authority figures had big mouths and went back and told your mom what you told them, too, so I just mostly wrote out my private thoughts, fears, and dreams in poetry and stories. I confided in a few friends, mostly the ones I discovered had families nearly as crazy as I thought mine was. It seems I was drawn to these people. When you read these stories, essays, and poems, I think that you'll probably agree that, it might be part of my genetic make-up, but I'm still drawn to "crazy" – and that's not necessarily a bad thing.

First of all, let me say that I'm not using the word "crazy" in a derogatory manner in this book. I'm using it as it was presented to me. A part of life. An attribute. "The girl's pretty." "The dog's lazy." "The house is old." "That man is crazy!" And crazy might mean a lot of different things. It might mean, literally, pertaining to a mental illness – i.e., "He was in the crazy house for years." Or it might mean quirky or different – i.e., "She was so bizarre, she was downright crazy." Or it might mean intense – i.e., "It was crazy fun to see them dance on Friday nights." It could even mean something in-between all of those other things. Then there's the clinical definition of crazy, and all of its social contexts.

Crazy is so many different things to so many different people. Say the word crazy to one person and you may see a smile pass her lips; say it to someone else and you may see him cry. It's a tough subject to address. Yet I've tackled it here, in several graces and guises. From a child who screams all the way to the operating room because she has changed her mind to a town made famous because it murdered innocent people; from an old man haunted by his life's bad deeds as he nears his end to a young mom pushed too far in defending her only child from another bullying child; from one who realizes she has to learn to forgive or be driven to a dark place to a delusional homeless man who may be more together than anyone realizes; from a high school girl determined to stick out a miserable basketball season to a college freshman who must decide whether she will remain the victim of date rape or become a survivor or maybe even something else by the time all is said and done. Other characters and their maladies to watch for include a 16-year-old girl who issues a warning because she feels like she's losing her grip and isn't sure what to do; someone who cries for something she can't name; a child who hates coloring; a 95-year-old woman on her birthday; a man apparently unsatisfied enough with his family life that he pulls up stakes and starts a second family in another state; a woodpecker that annoys a writer to no end (not exactly); a doe and buck singled out "in season;" an immobile would-be swimmer who cannot make it out of the murky waters. Some "characters" in these pages are inanimate objects – mountaintops explored and exploited; back roads that seem to come to life; a house folding under foreclosure; the feeling of shutting down annually when summer has gone. There is life; there is death. There is hatred and love. One love poem speaks of the shyness of feelings, that exuberance of love but being afraid to tell, being afraid of knowing, yet wanting fulfillment thereof. Three sets of song lyrics proclaim the beautiful insanity of a lifetime together in love, the pathways we may take in this world, and the lonely crowd (those who stand by and remember what happens in life, the storytellers and carriers, if you will). In the end, though, I believe there is always hope. If there wasn't hope, I wouldn't be here to write these pieces; I wouldn't be here to tell these stories. I am living proof of other people's hope, as well as of my own.

Running From Crazy. Mental illness. It's a concept that I spent a great portion of my life denying and pretending did not exist. Until I saw the incredibly real damage that such actions could cause to the person suffering from the "craziness," as well as those around him/her. I still run on occasion. But eventually, I stop, turn myself around, close my eyes, and embrace it. After all, we have to love ourselves before we can love anyone else.

CAP

I would be remiss if I did not take the time to thank and acknowledge the various publications/competitions which have previously published/acknowledged my work.

The poem "In the Spirit" appeared in the online journal Still, in

The poem "Late November Sky" originally in the 2012 *Clinch Mountain Review*, a literary review of Southwest Virginia.

"Please Don't Make Me Color" received 2nd Honorable Mention in the 2012 "Sometimes You Can't Be Saved From Yourself" contest of the Green River Writers.

The article "John Daniel Hash: Reconstructing a Life" originally appeared in the 2011 issue of *Our Grayson Heritage*, the annual publication of the Grayson County (Virginia) Heritage Foundation.

The poem "Mountaintops in Memories" appeared in Volume 16 of *Pine Mountain Sand & Gravel*.

The poems "Foreclosure" and "October Evening, Grayson County" were originally published in *Kudzu*, a publication of Hazard County Community College, the first in the 2012 edition and the latter in the 2013 edition.

"The 'ME' in Team" received 2nd place in the 2013 Jesse Stuart Prize in Young Adult Fiction and "Call It Paradise" received 3rd place in the 2013 Emma Bell Miles Prize for Essay, both awarded by Lincoln Memorial University.

"I Changed My Mind" received 1st place in Nonfiction for the 2013 contest of the Tennessee Mountain Writers.

The essay "Heart of the Matter: A Difference-Maker in My Life" received 1st place in the Prose Essay: Appreciation of Poetry category through the Poetry Society of Virginia. "Lifetime" received 3rd Honorable Mention in the PSV's annual contests for 2013, as well, in the "Come Out Swinging" lyrics contest.

"Call It Paradise" has appeared on Jan L. Frayne's "The Wounded Warrior" blog at http://whatislove-2010.blogspot.com/2013/09/call-it-paradise-by-writewaytogo.html

Stories: Fact and Fiction

I Changed My Mind — 1-6
Spirits — 8-14
Behind the Couch — 15-17
Call It Paradise — 19-41
Ghosts — 43-61
Heart of the Matter: A Difference-Maker in My Life — 63-66
Diner Dude — 67-79
The "Me" in Team — 81-88
John Daniel Hash: Reconstructing a Life — 89-105

Poetry: Lyrics and Verse

Warning: Message From a 16-Year-Old — 108-111
I Cried — 112
Mountaintops in Memories — 113-115
In the Spirit — 116-117
Gina and Tommy, Revisited: 2013 — 118-119
Lifetime (Lyrics) — 120-121
Hibernation — 122
In Season — 123
October Evening, Grayson County — 124
Blow Me Home — 125
Mary, Holding Court — 126-127
Please Don't Make Me Color — 128-129
Pathways (Lyrics) — 130-131
Poets Under the Skin — 132
Late November Sky — 133
Foreclosure — 134-135
Running From Crazy — 136-137
Tonight She Sleeps Alone — 138
Her — 139
Unable to Swim — 140-141
(The Memories of) The Lonely Crowd (Lyrics) — 142-143
Woodpecker — 144
A New Day Dawned — 145
About the Author/About the Cover Artist — 147-148

Contributing Artists/Photographers:

Kacper Lengiewicz was born in Poznan, Poland, in 1983. In 2005, he immigrated to London, where he continues to pour his ups and downs onto paper in the form of drawings. He is a Capoerista, lightbringer, and most of all… a regular guy like all of us.

Sarah Shaffer is a writer and a freelance editor and proofreader based in Seattle. She loves animals, the outdoors, and living simply. Find her at www.sarahshaffer.com and @sarahsshaffer (Twitter).

Pat Shrader is a photographer and sweet tea connoisseur. Read more about him in the "About the Author/About the Cover Artist" section on pages 136-137 or on the back cover. Also check out his work at www.BlueRidgeExpressions.com.

Special thanks also to **Patricia Hudson** and **LEAF** (Lindquist Environmental Appalachian Fellowship) for permission to use the photo accompanying the poem "Mountaintops in Memories." Find out more about LEAF at tnleaf.org

Stories: Fact and Fiction

(Chrissie Anderson, close to the age of learning that the "cool kids" might not have it all together, after all.)

1 Changed My Mind

"I changed my mind!" I screamed all the way out of my hospital room, my mother looking on, distressed. "I changed my mind!" I continued screaming down the hall, past the nurses' desk, past the waiting room, through the swinging double doors, and into the operating room. I watched as the lights overhead in the halls seemed to zoom past me and couldn't tell if they were moving or if I was. I could smell all the hospital smells, unlike any other place in the world, bleach and antiseptics. My breath caught in my throat as I heaved in air between crying and screaming, proclaiming to the world that my thoughts on this tonsillectomy had most definitely readjusted themselves...

It was 1977. I was in first grade and had been informed about this procedure by several classmates who had recently undergone it. They talked about how cool it was to get all the ice cream you wanted, to get gifts even though it wasn't Christmas or your birthday, to lay in a bed that you could move up and down with a button while watching TV with a similar contraption to change channels. I couldn't wait for the tonsillectomy because it would give me something in common with the "cool" kids at school.

Mom tried explaining to me that we weren't having our tonsils removed for any reason except that we needed them out. "We" meant both of us. Mom frequently got strep throat; by the age of six, I had developed pneumonia five times and double-pneumonia twice. Dr. Tolosa believed that having the tonsils removed would help each of us maintain better health. (Plus all the cool kids were having it done!)

The afternoon that we went to Dr. Tolosa's office for our final check-ups before being admitted to our hospital, I opened wide, said "ahhh," and then waited while Mom did the same.

"Ah, Dora," Dr. Tolosa began in his heavily Filipino-accented English. "Things do not look so good." He shined a little flashlight back into her throat and shook his head as he told her to close her mouth. "Not good. No operation for you tomorrow," he announced. "Christine is good to go, but not you."

I wanted to tell him that my name was Christin*a*, not Christine, but every time I asked Mom about it, she told me that it would be rude to correct him because he was one of my elders. If you asked me, it was pretty rude for him not to be able to get my name right after all the time I'd been going to his office. A few minutes later, we drove over to the hospital and they admitted me.

First off, the TV couldn't be turned on because the guys who did that had already left for the day. The remote control had nothing to work with, so I resigned myself to playing with the buttons that made the bed move up and down. I'd been sick so much that I knew every nurse in the hospital by name, including the ones in the ER. "Hi, Pat!" I greeted the first nurse who came into my room. "Can I have some ice cream?" I flashed my biggest smile and asked politely.

"Sorry, kiddo! No ice cream until *after* the tonsils come out."

I just looked at her. This was not going according to plan at all. First no TV, now no ice cream.

My grandparents came to see me and to say good night. "Chrissle," my grandfather addressed me by my nickname when the announcement came on that visiting hours were ending. "What can Papaw bring back for you tomorrow?"

Finally! Something would go as projected! "Oh, Papaw! I want a Baby This-N'-That! She's a big-girl doll. She can eat and talk on the phone!"

"Baby This-N'-That," he repeated aloud. "I'll see what I can do." He and Mamaw kissed me and left the room.

Mom read me a couple of bedtime stories, but I wasn't really tired. She tucked me in and kissed me. "Are you scared?"

I looked into her face, more than a little confused. Why would I be scared? I couldn't wait to get my ice cream and the baby doll, and for the TV to be turned on! She seemed relieved that I wasn't scared. (I didn't realize that I had reason to be!)

The next morning, bright and early, the TV guys made the TV work. I flipped channels while Mom brushed out my long brown hair. All was going perfectly until Pat came in with a big needle.

"Okay, kiddo, let's turn over and get a shot. This will help you sleep."

Sleep? Shot? Panic set in immediately. Why would I want to go to sleep? I just woke up! I turned in desperation to Mom, who obviously saw the fear on my face. She tried to sooth me as Pat rolled me over. I felt the painful needle prick my tender six-year-old butt and screamed as though someone had just shot me with a gun instead of a needle. "I changed my mind! I changed my mind!"

The next thing I knew, two men rolled in a table on wheels and moved me over to that and started rolling me out of the room, away from my mother. I reached out for her in anguish. Surely she would save me; after all, she was my mother and she had promised to go through this with me and then backed out! But she didn't; she watched me go with tears in her eyes. I had to make someone understand me. This was not what I had bargained for at all! "I changed my mind!" All the way down the hall, I continued to scream, thinking that surely someone, somewhere would rush to my aid; someone would help me. No one did.

In the operating room, I looked up to see Dr. Tolosa wearing a surgical mask. "Ah, Christine," he began.

Elder or not, I would not stand for being called the wrong name today. I screamed with all I had in me, "My – name – is – not – Christine; it's – Chris – tin –*a*!" I cried so hard that I had to take in gulps of air between each syllable.

It seemed that he smiled at my outrage and placed a mask over my mouth and nose. "Breathe deeply," he instructed.

"I – don't – want – to!" I yelled, sucking air in between each word.

I awoke in a strange room. Everything smelled too clean and it was so white that it hurt my eyes. I could feel something in my throat. For some reason, I had it in my head that it was one of those little patties of butter from the school cafeteria tray and I couldn't figure out *why* that was stuck in my throat, but I knew it shouldn't be. I reached my fingers in to try to pull it out and SMACK! Out of nowhere, a nurse I didn't know grabbed my hand and slapped it hard. "Don't do that again! You'll pull out your stitches." I gave up and cried once again, this time no sounds coming from my exhausted body.

Upon returning to my room, Mom hugged me. I didn't hug her back. She had betrayed me and I would not soon forgive her. I refused to watch TV. I refused to eat ice cream (or anything else for that matter). Papaw pulled a doll from behind his back. My joy turned to disgust as he handed over the Baby That-A-Way. Not the big girl baby that talked on the phone and fed herself, but the baby-baby that did nothing more significant than crawl and wiggle her butt. Nothing was as it should be. Nothing at all. The cool kids had gotten everything wrong.

(Drawing for "Spirits," by Kacper Lengiewicz, London, England)

Spirits

I had never traveled in New England; in fact, I hadn't traveled much at all beyond the states surrounding my home in Virginia. Having an Internet boyfriend from Boston changed all of that for a time. Greg wanted to show me everything in his world. I was certainly a willing participant in this grown-up game of show-and-tell. The English major in me adored going to the actual "House of Seven Gables" that inspired Hawthorne's novel; the Children's Librarian in me giggled at being photographed by the statues of McCloskey's *Make Way for Ducklings* at Boston Public Garden; the history buff in me thrilled to visiting the gravesites of "the Pilgrims," people I had read and studied about since my earliest grade school memories; and the general nerd in me completely dug the touristy things like visiting the Ocean Spray Cranberry World and the original bar where the TV series *Cheers* had been taped. All the places we visited took on an inexplicable spirit of fun and adventure – for me, because it was like storybook tales come-to-life, and for Greg, because he got to teach me all about the places he had visited as a kid and largely took for granted. It was this same wide-eyed wonderment that led to my first encounter with Salem, Massachusetts, in Autumn 1999. In the spirit of fun and adventure, thrown together with a dash of seasonal spookiness, Greg and I made our way to Salem, Massachusetts – "The City of Witches."

For hours after arriving, we ambled along the streets looking at cleverly-named shops, all seemingly pertaining to witchcraft and the occult. I soon learned that Salem had as many psychics, haunted houses, and witch museums as my little hometown back in Appalachia had banks, pharmacies, and churches. I talked Greg into going into two or three of the witch museums, all more or less alike, trying to give an accurate historic accounting of what had occurred in Salem, but each also attempting to put its own spin on the tragedy in order to stand out from the other museums in town. I knew most of the stories, as I had always been interested in the Witchcraft Trials and had even done my junior research paper in high school on witchcraft (which displeased and alarmed my mother to no end, at the time). I was disappointed to learn that Gallows Hill wasn't exactly in walking distance, as I would have found it fascinating to visit there on this trip, too.

Outside of the witch museums, the carnival-like atmosphere resumed and I picked up postcards and trinkets galore for friends and family members back home. Greg and I took pictures of shop fronts, costumed tourists, and various other interesting sights. I had lost count of how many witch costumes I'd seen since arriving. I'd observed everything from cheap plastic masks and capes to authentic-looking Victorian dresses and shoes. The time and money spent on even the tiniest details of some of the costumes was mind-boggling. The dedication to their costumes was beyond doubt or reproach. Salem brought people-watching to a whole new level!

After the sun sank low in the sky and the moon had begun its ascent, we ventured out on the edge of town, just holding hands, talking, and planning for the future. I can't remember exactly what made me look behind us suddenly, but I did and saw three big guys following us. They looked like teens, but I couldn't be sure in the mostly-dark evening. I whispered to Greg that we were being followed. It quickly became evident that he wasn't going to be very helpful in this situation as he was obviously more terrified than I was. I stopped walking and heard the sound of footsteps crunching in the gravel behind us. We had somehow ventured far from the light-hearted witch-lined streets of the actual town and were in a deserted area without sidewalks or streetlights. I wheeled around and Greg stepped not in front of me to protect me, but behind me, cowering.

I demanded that the three guys tell us why they were following us. "Nice camera," one of them commented, pointing to my then-stylish 35 mm.

Greg's voice quavered as he whispered, "Give it to them!"

"Thanks," I answered calmly. "You can get one at Wal-Mart. That's where I got mine." I took a step towards them, one against three, one completely non-muscular twenty-something woman against three teenage punks who looked like something straight out of Gold's Gym. Greg remained where he had stopped, now a couple of yards from where I stood. I looked into the eyes of all three of them and spoke to the one who had made the comment about my camera. "I think it's a good time for you to stop following us. It's only gonna get you in trouble." Then, without turning to look behind me, I said to my cowardly boyfriend, "Come on, let's go."

Greg practically ran past me, terrified. I didn't walk too fast. My knees felt like gelatin, but I refused to display any degree of fear. I strode as calmly as possible back toward the lights, back toward the sounds of laughter and fun. I didn't look behind me, but I also heard no footsteps following us.

Once back in the boundary of safety in the busier streets of town, Greg stopped and wiped sweat from his forehead and upper lip. I was rather surprised that he hadn't wet himself, to be quite honest. I was way past disgusted with his lack of courage and inability to even pretend to be able to protect us. Looking back, it was the first step towards what was thankfully an inevitable break-up.

"You can't do that," he told me, still visibly shaken from the whole encounter. "You'll get hurt!"

"Yeah, well, I'd rather get hurt standing up for myself than from running or just giving street punks like them what they want, Greg!"

And I looked around me realizing that the spell had been utterly, completely, and undeniably broken. In the time since we had been followed out of the lights and luster of the place until we arrived back, somehow miraculously unscathed, the whole town had transformed. The giddiness had turned to ghoulishness; the frivolity had migrated to foolishness. The carnival I enjoyed for several hours had shut down and given way to something cheap, ugly, and undesired. I announced to Greg that I was ready to leave. And I was. And I never wanted to return.

My mind drifted back to April 20, earlier that same year. Columbine, Colorado, the site of the worst high school massacre in United States history. A horrible tragedy masterminded by two outsiders who grew tired of being outcasts, tired of being bullied because they were different. Without taking up for what those two boys did to innocent classmates, a scenario suddenly occurred to me as we got back into Greg's car and left Salem behind. Tourism at Salem rested firmly on the backbone of a tragedy – the tragic persecution of innocent people when an entire culture succumbed to mass hysteria, and twenty people – likely innocent of any wrongdoings, let alone being practitioners of witchcraft – died because they were different. Columbine was still fresh in our nation's history.

What if someone, someday, decided that it would be good for that local economy to build an amusement park on the site where Columbine's own thirteen martyrs died? That spirit of adventure I'd arrived in Salem with had vanished; I left town feeling ashamed for partaking in the spirit of fun that was founded on the spirit of mayhem that cost twenty people their lives, and I wept for having done so.

Behind the Couch

My cousin Mindy and I grabbed our cousin Melody and dashed behind the couch in the apartment where Mindy and her family lived, about thirty minutes from Detroit.

Melody and I were visiting with our mothers, both sisters of Mindy's father, my Uncle Buddy. Mindy and I were four years old, and Melody was three. Mindy's little brother Josh was two and thrived on picking on Melody. He had a real talent for making her miserable and enjoyed doing so because he could make her cry so easily.

Melody's mother, my Aunt Janie, had a temper. To be fair, everyone in the family had a temper. She kept telling Mindy's mom (Brandy), that Josh needed to quit bothering Melody. Brandy smacked his bottom a couple of times, but he delighted in hearing Melody wail.

It seemed like the typical family argument. I had certainly heard enough of those that I knew there would be screaming and angry crying, name-calling, probably some door-slamming, and then things would calm down. But not that night in Michigan.

Janie stormed into the living room, pushing Melody out of Josh's reach, grabbing her purse. At first, I thought she was taking her purse and leaving. Instead, she pulled something small from it – a gun.

Mindy must have seen it at the same time I did. We knew better than to get in the middle of that, so we grabbed Melody and quickly crawled behind the couch, Melody sitting between us, as we prepared to protect her from either side. A large window sat behind us. I felt cold air seeping in, but knew that wasn't the reason for our shaking.

"Janie!" my mother yelled. "Put that thing away! We don't need this kind of trouble!"

Janie screamed, "I told her to keep her little monster away from my baby! I told her to make him stop! If she won't stop him, *I will!*"

Mindy and I looked at each other, suddenly realizing that we had grabbed Melody, but had no idea where Josh was. I peeked around the corner of the couch and saw Janie wildly waving the gun in the air, shouting at Brandy, wide-eyed and screechy. Josh stood at the edge of the hallway, confused and terrified. Mindy must have been looking out from her end of the couch, too, because I heard her call out to her little brother, "Run, Josh! Run to your bedroom!"

Janie turned to see us duck back to our hiding place. Mindy and I each put our arms around Melody and waited while our mothers argued more quietly. Janie's voice came closer, and then stopped. She looked behind the couch and saw us three girls huddling, crying. Silently, she reached for Melody. Mindy and I refused to let her touch her own daughter. Then Janie started crying and apologized.

Melody reached for her and Janie pulled her from our protective arms, flung open the door and stomped out into the nighttime, waiting for Mom and me to meet her at Mom's car and an unexpected nighttime drive back to Virginia.

(Photo of Chrissie Anderson and Melissa Little as children, on their Mamaw Little's couch)

Call It Paradise

There I am again, that same dream. I am in Carl's friend's dorm room, over in Hillman Hall. There's a Janet Jackson video playing silently in the background, the newest video from her *Rhythm Nation* album in October 1989. It's the one where they're all in army-like mode. The video in its odd black-and-white taping adds to the surreal nature of everything else that happened that night.

Nothing happened the way that it was supposed to. The fact that I went to Hillman to go to a party up on the third floor with Gabe Wilson, but I somehow ended up with some guy named Carl in his friend's room on the first floor. The fact that I'd only had alcohol once before in my life – the previous weekend at a Homecoming party up on Treasure Mountain, delivered with discretion by a good friend with no ulterior motives – and then tonight I'd just taken up the challenge to drink this Bacardi 151 ("It's like Bacardi times ten," Carl's friend had laughed) and shot it back like it was nothing, because it tasted like nothing, until I tried to stand up and then the world started spinning like a tilt-a-whirl that I couldn't make stop. The fact that Gabe came looking for me and Carl and his friend told me to be very quiet, like we were playing some sort of game, and I'd gone along with it, not really because I thought it would be fun, but because I don't think I could even talk. The fact that Gabe, God bless his sweet soul, then tried climbing into the room through the window from outside, short little Gabe, and something inside me thought I was still on the third floor and I thought, "Oh, God, he's gonna fall off the ledge and kill himself and it'll all be my fault," and I gasped really loudly and sucked air in until I nearly passed out, completely falling out of my chair and falling onto the lower bunk of the two beds in the dorm room where all of this took place, and hitting my head on the painted cinder block wall and thinking, "Wow, I'll bet that hurt," yet not feeling a thing. The fact that I kept seeing that video and thinking how militant it was, how completely unromantic the song was even though the music wasn't even audible, how unlike my lifelong expectations for my first time this was all going to be. Because I knew somehow that we were going to have sex, this Carl guy and me. He kept kissing me, caressing me. Yet I felt none of it. I kept wondering how it could possibly happen this way. I hadn't necessarily been saving my virginity for someone "special," but God, I at least wanted to be present in body for it, you know?

Then I see myself lying down on the bed. I'm wearing that pretty blue sweater with the delicate little white hearts on it and a pair of blue jeans. I love that sweater. It actually looks good on me. I'm eighteen years old and don't have the most positive body image in the world. Hell, what eighteen-year-old girl does? Especially one who has been fat her whole life? I weighed ninety-nine pounds in third grade. When I had my physical done the summer before starting college, the doctor who did mine felt my breasts and proclaimed, "You'd never know if you had breast cancer or not, your breasts are so lumpy!" That's exactly what a girl who has never even been felt up wants to hear, you know? No self-esteem. I have a pretty enough face, I think, though I won't go anywhere without make-up. Or without styling my long, spiral-permed brown hair – and teasing the front way up (remember, it's the late 80's and the higher the hair, the closer you are to God). But the rest of me… The rest of me, I've never been so sure about. And I could never ask my mother. We don't talk about sex. Or anything remotely sexual in nature – which is ironic, now that I think of it. The first record she ever bought for me, when I was probably around four or five years old, was by the British band Hot Chocolate and was called "You Sexy Thing." Flash forward to early 1985, a typical Saturday when I'm cleaning house while blasting music on the stereo, listening to the latest album by another British band, Duran Duran. "Save A Prayer" finishes playing and my mother lifts the needle from the record and asks, "Do you know what that song is about?" Well, let me think here… The lyrics go: *Some people call it a one-night stand/ But we can call it Paradise…* I smile in the dreamy way that all thirteen-year-old girls smile when smitten by lust and answer, "Yeah, isn't it cool?" But that was just a thirteen-year-old girl in lust with five hot guys from the UK, not a drunk, first-semester college girl who can't even feel her limbs, trying to figure out what the hell is happening and how to have an active role in it.

I'm suddenly aware of Carl fumbling with the zipper on my jeans. Holy crap, this is really going to happen! I remember going to the movies with Bobby Dunford and swatting his hands to try to make him watch *A Fish Called Wanda*. I knew Bobby Dunford and I liked Bobby Dunford. He never asked me out again. I know almost nothing about this Carl guy except that I think he said he was a football player. Yes, he must be a football player; he's wearing his room key on a shoe string around his neck like all the football players do. Why do they do that? Don't they know how stupid it makes them look?

One hand slides up under my sweater, cupping my doctor-proclaimed lumpy breasts, groping them eagerly, while his other hand begins working its way into my unzipped jeans. I squeeze my eyes shut. Then I'm acutely aware of his erection pushing against my backside, through my jeans. Why can I feel that, but not my legs? I try to move. Maybe I can get up and leave. But I still can't feel my legs. My arms, too, feel as heavy and useless as lead. And my mouth won't work – no voice comes out. Maybe some mumbles or indiscernible noises, but who knows what this guy is taking any of that to mean? I definitely feel his fingers make their way inside my panties. I have to do something. I must do something. Something. Something. Anything...

And I'm awake. That is where I wake up every single night. I wake up at that point in the dream, crying. On the nights when my beautiful party-hearty roommate Martha Lee is there, she comes over to my bed and asks if I'm okay. As though I am still paralyzed, stuck in the dream, I shake my head, no voice coming out through my sobs.

I honestly don't remember the sex. I just know that it happened. I know for a few reasons. I know because Carl's friend completely went off when Carl snuck me out of the room to take me back over to my own dorm – because I'd "fucked up his sheets." I remember looking back and thinking, "Dear God, someone must be bleeding to death." Maybe I was hallucinating; maybe in that intoxicated state everything seemed more intense than it actually was. I really don't know. I just remember thinking that whoever was bleeding like that surely needed medical attention. Carl, being the *gentleman* that he was, walked me to my car, which was actually parked in the Chapel parking lot, near my dorm. Never mind that he had a car right there in the parking lot behind the building where we had been. Besides, the fresh air would help me sober up faster. I remember that I had to pee. I had to pee desperately. I didn't care where. At this point, was dignity really at stake? So I lowered my jeans and panties and peed against a weeping willow that stood next to the Duck Pond. I remember thinking something along the lines of "Weeping willow, cry for me, 'cos I just don't have the strength right now!" But I'm still not sure if I was lamenting or joking when I thought it.

Carl took my car keys, unlocked the door for me, put me in the passenger seat, got in and drove me around for a while. I have no idea where or for how long. After the drive, he found a parking spot behind my dorm, MaWa, and walked me to the main door of the building. No goodbye kiss or anything like that. He handed my keys back and said, "I'll see you tomorrow."

I looked at the entrance to the building, thinking it simultaneously seemed like the open jaws of a monster and a landing pad to home, a feeling that I would have hundreds more times in my four years at Emory & Henry, for various reasons. I took a deep breath and tried my best to look sober as I walked through the main door. In case you have never tried to look sober, here is something you should know: *the more sober you try to look, the drunker you obviously appear to everyone else in the world.* As this was my first time being drunk, however, I didn't realize this very important rule of the universe yet.

When I walked in, there sat a resident advisor and the Residence Director of Women. I must have looked like hell. Both of them stopped the game of cards they were playing and stared at me, just short of having their jaws drop open. The resident advisor spoke first. "Are you okay, Chelsea?"

Stay cool. Stay calm. "I'm fine." I answered a little more shakily than I would have liked, but I got it out without breaking down.

Then the Residence Director of Women spoke. "If you need to talk or anything –"

"I'm fine, thanks. Just tired." And so it was set. The tough act was on. The mask was placed. And denial had set in that anything "wrong" had happened at all. I was the one who had made a bad decision and I would now deal with those consequences. Whatever the hell that might mean.

I took the elevator to the fourth floor and walked all the way to the end of the hall, and then to the end of the "short-L" where my room was. I never locked my door, something I was glad for tonight, this morning, whatever it was by now. My answering machine was blinking. Gabe had left a message sometime after midnight asking if I was okay. How could I ever hope to explain any of this to him? I couldn't. I wouldn't. Not ever.

I started to undress, but caught my reflection in the floor-length mirror and lost control of my emotions. With my sweater half-on and half-off, I just stood there sobbing. I didn't want to see my reflection and thanked God when my vision became so blurry that I could no longer see any part of who I was. I didn't know this new person standing there and she didn't know me. She was not the same person who had waited for Simon LeBon to whisk her away to that promised Paradise of "Save A Prayer" that he sang about when she was thirteen; she was some girl who had just had sex with a guy she barely knew – while she was drunk – and all she knew for sure was that there was nothing Paradisiacal about the place she was standing in right now.

About five minutes later, once I'd flung myself down on the bed, glad that Martha Lee was gone for the weekend and that I didn't have to explain anything to her, my stomach began churning. I still hadn't managed to get into my pajamas completely, just into the bottoms. I knew what was coming next. The shame of what had happened was not to be enough. No, God was going to punish me righteously. I ran down the hall to the bathrooms, barged into a stall, and hurled like I had never hurled before. The acidic taste of the Bacardi 151 filled my mouth, my nostrils, and flew like projectile missiles from my face. I hugged the toilet with what strength I had regained in my upper extremities. "Really, God?" I wanted to shout. "Is all of *this* necessary, too?" I looked down at that gorgeous blue sweater with the little white hearts on it. Puke covered the front. *How appropriate*, I remember thinking. *It's just like me. Stained. I'll never love it again, either.*

By the time I left the bathroom, I was too weak to walk. I literally crawled back to my room. I took off the sweater and balled it up, throwing it into the corner, as far away from my view and range of smell as I could. I'd wash it when I had more strength. Or maybe I'd throw it away; if only I could do the same to myself…

Martha Lee and another friend woke me up when they got back around 4:00 on Sunday afternoon. I still felt like hell. I described the tremendous headache, the vomiting, the "wanting to crawl somewhere and die" feelings. Martha Lee grinned and surmised, "This is your first hangover, isn't it?" I wanted to be sarcastic with her, but realized that she was the most worldly person I knew and that I probably needed to be nice to her, that I might need to ask her questions about some of this at some point. So I simply answered yes.

"Where was the party? Were there hot guys there?" Her eyes brightened as she pummeled me with questions.

I told her about the party and skipped as many details as possible about the rest, saying only that I ended up drinking with some guy and that we had sex. Her eyes got wide, as did the other friend's. Then she smiled really big. "Chelsea Anderson – got drunk and had sex?" It was like it was some miraculous thing, like one of the Seven Signs or something. "What's his name?"

"Carl," I answered. "No clue what his last name is. Football player."

On a campus of fewer than 1000 students, the two of them figured out who he was pretty quickly. "He's in my comp class," the friend volunteered. I pretended to follow their chitchat, but I honestly didn't care.

I was relieved when 4:45 rolled around and it was time to get ready to go to the cafeteria for dinner. Little did I know that mealtime would never be the same for me again.

My head still pounded and I felt like I was looking at the world through something other than my own contact lenses. Nothing felt right. Nothing looked right. Things sounded different. I felt like everyone was watching me. And maybe they were. I looked around, suddenly not sure of what Carl or his friend even looked like. Less than twenty-four hours had passed and I was either already blocking it out or forgetting it. Either way, I was kinda thankful for the memory lapse. However, it took me all of five minutes in the cafeteria to realize that, just because *I* hadn't made it to brunch that day, certainly did not mean that stories from the night before hadn't made it on my behalf in living color.

I got the blandest thing to eat that I possibly could – cereal. As I stood there waiting for the milk to come out of the dispenser, a guy walked up and touched me on the shoulder. I jumped. "Hey," he said quietly. "It's me, Carl."

"Oh, yeah, hi," I mumbled.

"I didn't see you at brunch," he said nonchalantly, as he got a glass of milk.

"No, I wasn't much feeling up to coming over here. And I was working on some homework," I lied, not wanting him to think that I was in any way inconvenienced by anything that had transpired the night before.

"Well, I just wanted to make sure you were okay. I'll see you around."

And that was it. I'll see you around. Which I totally understood. *I've done my part. I've checked on you. You're alive. You're okay. We're finished here.*

I went to my usual table in the back corner and sat down with my friends, all of whom were careful about asking how I was, how my weekend had been, what I had done last night, etc. It was like seeing the proverbial elephant in the room, only the elephant was me. Or rather, what I'd done. Everyone knew, or knew some part of it, and probably wanted to know more. They were waiting to see if I would tell more or if they were going to need to pry it out of me, or if they would have to wait for tidbits from somewhere else. I offered nothing of substance. It had been my stupidity and I would deal with it. I wasn't ready to share it with the world just yet, even if the world was more than eager to hear about it.

After downing my second bowl of cereal, I took my tray up to dump it. I took my usual route, not even realizing that it would take me by the table where Carl and his friends sat. Maybe I should go a different way. Why, though? For Pete's sake, we're all adults here. Judging from the snickers, guffaws, and stifled laughter, I gave the friends too much credit. Well, screw them; *I* was an adult. I wasn't changing my life just because they were immature cretins!

The dream started that night. It didn't get very far before I forced myself to wake up. I didn't want to remember. Remembering was going to be bad. Remembering was going to be some kind of ugly that I was not yet prepared to face. I refused to go back to sleep. I couldn't take the chance of ending up there again.

To say that the next few weeks were long ones would be an understatement. One day the week after it all transpired, I stopped in at the student health center on campus, or as we called it back in the day, the Infirmary. It had been four days and I was still bleeding. I didn't know if that was normal or not; I had no frame of reference and was not about to ask Martha Lee. Donna, the nurse, took me back into her office and closed the door. I'll never forget how nice and unobtrusively she dealt with the entire situation. "Was this your first time?" I set my jaw hard to keep all of my emotions in check and nodded my head. "Did your boyfriend use a condom?" Again I nodded my head, but inside, I set off into panic mode. My boyfriend – what a joke! Had he used a condom? I had no clue! How was I supposed to figure out *that* piece of the puzzle? My mind whirled around all of the horrible things that could result from the absence of a condom while sweet Donna was trying to explain to me that I had probably just torn some and that, if I continued bleeding, I should probably go to a doctor, just to be on the safe side. I must have had that deer-in-headlights look as I thanked her and started to leave, though, because she stopped me with just a gentle touch to my arm. "Was there alcohol involved? Chelsea, was the sex consensual?"

Words spilled out quickly. "No, I consented." No turning back now. "It was stupid on my part, but I knew what I was doing." I thought I saw her shake her head as I left, but I didn't turn back to see for sure.

The next day, I called Carl and asked if he had worn a condom. He acted for all the world like my phone call had inconvenienced him to no end. How dare I even bother him with such petty matters? Of course he had worn a condom. What kind of idiot did I think he was? Why had I gone to the Infirmary? I didn't tell them I was drunk, did I? *No, Carl,* I wanted to say. *I just told them I was stupid...*

When rumors fly on a small campus, it's a special kind of hell for the person or people caught up in the tales. Friends delicately began asking me questions about the things they were hearing. One night when I was working switchboard, my friend Harold was working sign-in, a thankless, mindless task where guys were required to leave a license, ID, or keys and sign-in to indicate which young lady they were going to visit (her name, room number and phone extension). During a few moments of quiet for both of us, he looked at me with a grave expression and said, "Are you doing okay?"

By now, it had been a couple of weeks. I was getting pretty good at dealing with this particular question on the outside. I had actually just about perfected my response. "Oh, Harold, I'm fine. It was a crazy night. I got way too drunk, had sex with someone I didn't know, and life goes on, you know?" I could even say it with a painted-on smile by this point.

But Harold didn't buy it. "You can call it what you want to, but you were raped."

My eyes darted around the vicinity, praying no one else had heard what he said. I glared at him. "No, Harold, you didn't hear what I said."

"I heard what you said. And I heard what Carl's friend said. And none of it really matters because what they did was wrong. They intentionally got you drunk and then Carl took advantage of you. In Virginia, that is rape. Plain and simple."

I wanted to reach across the switchboard box and slap Harold. I wanted to shake him hard and tell him no! I wanted to tell him that he couldn't talk about it that way, like it was just that way. Then what he had said registered. *I heard what Carl's friend said.* "His friend is talking about it?"

"All over the place, Chelsea. All about how he had to change the sheets after you guys finished, about —"

I held up my hand for him to stop. I really didn't want to hear any more. They really were talking about me. And they really were laughing at me in the cafeteria. At every single meal. It didn't matter what I said. It didn't matter how I tried to handle what had happened, internally or externally. Perception was going to go against me completely. I had been lying to everyone. Including myself. And all for absolutely nothing.

Harold was talking again. I had missed the first part of it, but he had pulled his chair closer, so that our conversation was not being broadcast all over the second-floor lounge of MaWa. "I know that it can't be an easy thing to deal with. And I know it sounds weird, but if you want a friend to go with you to talk to someone, I'll go with you. You need to report this. To someone."

I blinked unresponsively and looked past Harold, shaking my head. "No, the time for that is past. I can't go back there now." And I really didn't believe I could. Plus the fact remained that I honestly did not want to.

I began skipping more and more meals. It wasn't worth the daily walk of shame that I had to endure in going anywhere near Carl's circle of friends in the cafeteria. I even skipped classes occasionally and didn't go out as much on the weekends. The dream was becoming more and more intense each time I had it, so I slept less and less. I realized one day that I had truly hit rock bottom. Not eating, not sleeping, constantly lying about major facets of my existence... These were not healthy behaviors. On the nights when I did accidentally doze off, I would wake up thrashing under the covers or making horrific noises that woke up Martha Lee, who, in turn, would rush to my bed to wake me up and make sure I was okay. Yes, even Martha Lee, party girl extraordinaire, knew that something was amiss. "Chelsea, you need to talk to someone. This has been going on since you had sex with that Carl guy. I don't like the stories I've heard and you need to do *something*."

I needed to do something. Something. That was the problem. The one thing that I wanted to do was to die. I wanted it all to end. I'm not saying that I wanted to kill myself, though; that is an entirely different feeling and I have, at different times in my life, felt that way, too. But I just wanted everything to cease. If things couldn't cease, then I wanted them to somehow go back to a way that they had (I also realized), never truly been.

I spent the entirety of that day, literally, curled up in a ball in the closet of our dorm room. Something had to change that day. I had gone as low as I could go. And the way I saw it, I had two choices from which to go on: I could either stay curled up in that ball and give up or I could start rebuilding and I could rebuild in such a way that I could become the person I had always wanted to be. I didn't have to be that insecure eighteen-year-old with a negative body image, always doubting herself and every decision that she made. I didn't have to be trapped any longer because that other shell was beyond broken down – it was irreparable and a new abode needed to be created for a new me. I might have given away a part of me that I wasn't ready to say goodbye to, but that didn't mean I couldn't still look for Paradise!

Building a new you can be fun, but it also isn't easy, especially when the "you" that you're attempting to create is an ideal that the poet in you likens to a phoenix rising from the ashes of a former self. The fun part, though, is that you get to try out totally new things, kinda like buying a new wardrobe after a substantial weight loss. Let's see how this feels when I try it on; maybe this color will work out better than that last one. There are boundaries, but you don't know what they are until you reach them. Each day is a new adventure in exploring who you are becoming, in who you really are. And that is more exciting than words can accurately describe!

That doesn't mean that there aren't plenty of days, though, when you hit a snag in the building process, or when the proposed blueprint doesn't suffer a setback or two. A dinner or two when the guffawing of his friends doesn't just set your teeth on edge and you want to do something horrible to each and every one of them, when you want to stand up on a table in the middle of the cafeteria and tell your side of the story, even if it *was* your own stupidity that landed you in that situation…

Day by day, though, I felt better; I felt stronger. I reveled in who I was becoming. I welcomed her and was likewise welcomed by her. I had never known self-acceptance like this before. The people who knew me and loved me didn't care what Carl and his cronies spread around campus. My friends embraced me and made sure I wasn't in a situation like that again, just like the new me did – no drinking with strangers, no wandering off from the group. What had happened was bad, but I did learn a lot from it. Lessons learned the hard way tend to stick best, I guess.

The semester wound down. The Saturday night of finals, just a week or so before Christmas, snow fell in our little world nestled deep in the mountains of southwestern Virginia. And at Emory & Henry, that meant one thing: sledding on the golf course! Well, to be perfectly fair, it also meant a substantial amount of drinking and general socializing. Still needing to study for an exam or two, and needing to wrap my last few gifts for friends at school, as well as family members at home, I decided to hang out in the dorm, but to leave my door standing open and enjoy the holiday chaos up and down the hallway. Two friends, Brian and Donnie, stopped by, their cheeks and noses red with "holiday merriment" (and likely some high-quality bourbon), and I invited them in. No sooner had they sat down than my telephone rang. I picked up in my usual manner. "Yeah?"

At the other end, there was a slight pause and then the sound of static, like a tape recorder starting up. And then a male voice, obviously on a tape recorder of some sort, announced, "This is one of Carl's friends and I'm just wondering if you're really as cheap as he says you are."

I threw the phone down, as though it had suddenly turned into a serpent in my hand. I turned quickly and ran from the room, my entire world suddenly skewed and falling apart, the ground was peeling away beneath my feet. I fell in the hall and pulled myself up against the wall. How dare them! How could they do this to me after weeks and weeks of me not giving a damn and showing them and the rest of the world that I didn't care anymore, that they couldn't hurt me anymore, that I was stronger than anything that they could throw my way? I sat there sobbing, rocking back and forth with my knees pulled tight against my chest, Brian and Donnie now beside me asking what had just happened. Before anyone else could get a chance to see me that way, they helped me to my feet and took me back into my room, closing the door. Brian reached into my refrigerator and pulled out a Mountain Dew, handed it to me, and asked again what happened. I finally pulled myself together enough to tell them about the voice on the other end of the phone. Although I'd never discussed what had happened on that October night with either of these guys, I could tell that they, too, had heard the stories.

"Did you recognize the voice?"

I really didn't know any of Carl's friends personally, but I had heard enough of the jeers for long enough that I was fairly certain of the voice. But I couldn't prove anything. Brian and Donnie, though, were friends in the truest sense of the word – and drunk red necks, to boot – who were not about to let someone treat one of their friends that way. They made their way back to Hillman, going room to room searching for a tape recorder, but never found one.

I sat there the rest of the night, watching the phone in terror, as though it were a living, breathing organism, capable of harming me. Watching the phone gave way to nodding off, and the dream was back again, more vivid, more in-depth. I started to remember something important. Then the phone woke me up. I couldn't decide which was worse – the phone ringing or the dream. So I just sat there in silence, looking at it. The clock on the wall read 12:30. It was daylight outside. The answering machine kicked on; I held my breath and waited. "Hey, it's Lynne. Are you going to brunch?"

I grabbed the phone and made up an excuse not to go. "I'm trying to pack up stuff so I can get out of here right after my two exams tomorrow. I'm just ready to get the hell out of Dodge, you know," I tried to be breezy.

"I heard about your phone call last night."

"How the hell did you hear about that?"

"Donnie's dating Cassie. I saw her in the bathroom this morning and she told me about it. Don't let them tear you down again, Chelsea. You've come too far. This semester is almost over. See it through."

She was right. I owed it to my new self to do that much. The foundation of the person I had become was strong enough to handle the test; I felt certain of that, but I needed to walk into that cafeteria and prove it. I had to face down the cowards who had pulled the phone prank to let them know that they did not have the upper hand in this or any other matter that involved me. Not today, not ever again.

The first night of Christmas break, I lie alone in my own bed, back home in Tazewell. It is cold in my room, like it always is in winter. There is frost on the windows and I scratch my initials onto the glass, *CIA*. Home doesn't feel much like home tonight, though. This new me cannot seem to settle down here. The old me wasn't happy here, so I don't know why I thought the new version could thrive here at all. But this bedroom is still mine, it is still me; it is still my hideaway and safe place. The posters of Duran Duran have been replaced by some other rock band, probably a couple of rock bands since the Fab Five plastered the walls. But I close my eyes and remember that time. I still have the same boom-box. I still sleep on the same pillows in the same Holly Hobbie pillow cases (although I keep another pillow case over those now). I am at peace in this one room and I drift off to sleep in the one place where I know that nothing bad in the world can or will happen to me…

I'm suddenly aware of Carl fumbling with the zipper on my jeans. Yes, the dream. Again. One hand slides up under my sweater, cupping my doctor-proclaimed lumpy breasts, groping them eagerly, while his other hand begins working its way into my unzipped jeans. I squeeze my eyes shut. Then I'm acutely aware of his erection pushing against my backside, through my jeans. Why can I feel that, but not my legs? I try to move. Maybe I can get up and leave. But I still can't feel my legs. My arms, too, feel as heavy and useless as lead. And my mouth won't work – no voice comes out. Maybe some mumbles or indiscernible noises, but who knows what this guy is taking any of that to mean? I definitely feel his fingers make their way inside my panties. I have to do something. I must do something. Something. Something. Anything… And in one final attempt to do anything, I see myself in that dorm room in Hillman. As if in an out-of-body experience, I see the inebriated me who cannot feel my body somehow manage to turn over onto my stomach and I hear myself utter one word and one word alone: *"No!"* And then I see Carl flip me onto my back as though I am nothing but a rag doll and everything goes pitch black.

But it is enough. I know what really happened. I know what I have not allowed myself to remember for two long months. I know that Harold was right and that my gut was right and that I have lied to myself and to everyone else. And while I'm not sure what in God's name I am to do with any of that, I know that I am free from it. I know that I am terrified, but liberated. And even though I know that I will not report it, because I will not put myself through it over and over again – for I am now finished with it and this dream is forbidden to keep me awake any more nights – I will call Carl when I get back to campus after Christmas break. I will call him and tell him that I finally remembered and I will ask him what gave him the right to do what he did, what gave him the right to rape me. And when he tells me that it is *my* fault because *I* kissed *him*, I will ask him what kind of twisted son of a bitch he is. But I will not hate him because hating him will mean that he wins. No one will ever have that power over me again.

Ghosts

Elijah Miller was a sad old man. Reny, his wife of 50-plus years, had died five long months earlier. Cancer had finally done what he hadn't managed to do in all those years of marriage. He didn't really expect anyone to believe him, much less to understand him, but that woman had meant more to him than any other person he had ever known. He still wondered why she put up with his hell-raising ways for all those years. Believing it to be pure, unconditional love might be flattering himself too much, he decided. Whatever it was likely wedged somewhere between being duty-bound to the vows they exchanged in November 1926 and necessity, seeing as how her daddy hated Elijah and wouldn't let her come home after she married him anyway.

Now that she was gone, he replayed life-long scenarios in his mind almost continuously. He tried to remember if he had, even once in their married life, told Reny that he loved her. That notion sickened him, evoking the sense of something tasting like rotted meat stuck deep in his craw, somewhere he couldn't reach to pluck it out. It made him feel something he couldn't exactly describe, something crossed between fear, regret, and outright self-loathing at the realization that even if he had *told* her, he certainly had never *shown* her that he cared for her above all others. In fact, he had done plenty of the exact opposite.

He allowed the past to take him back to the beginning of their marriage. *Let's see, starting with our first*

Christmas, I went against her express desire to stay home and spend time with her alone to go on a turkey hunt with friends and kinfolk. That same day, I killed my brother-in-law, Frankie – yes, on Christmas Day. I put her through the hell of a trial where everyone in the town and county knew that she was now married to a murderer, and then was sentenced to the state penitentiary. Somehow, my employers at the mines sprang me after just a year, but I went right back to the liquor and all of my meanness. I beat her for no reason when I was drunk; I called her names and wore away her spirit as much as I could, 'cos I couldn't stand to think that she might be stronger than me. So I reckon I felt like I had to overpower her however I could. What a fool! I might have beat her down physically, and I sure tried to break her spirit, but a good person is good through and through, and there's no changing that if the person is set on staying true to herself. He tried to stop this line of thinking now, for he knew where it would lead; Elijah Miller had been down this road many times, most of them since Reny had gone to be with the Lord.

Today was his birthday. He turned 72 today. Seventy-two and pretty much alone. Sure, two of their daughters lived close enough that they came to visit often, Agatha and her man Josh just about every day. They were good to him, he knew. Josh was retired from Ford Motor Company up in Detroit, Michigan, and helped Elijah out on his farm daily now that Elijah had gotten too old to do much beyond taking stock of his earthly possessions in the field behind the farmhouse. Josh would often come up and walk with him, letting Elijah bend his ear with stories of his boyhood and the deeds he had done throughout his lifetime, sometimes trying to defend his actions and sometimes just speaking them aloud to get it all off his chest. Josh listened to the stories, Elijah knew and, unlike most people, when Josh stopped him to ask a question about the people, the places, or the circumstances, Elijah would take time to explain what he could. Josh shot straight with Elijah and the old man appreciated this. Josh didn't sugar-coat how he perceived things with Elijah, but he also didn't get all judgmental and self-righteous with his father-in-law. Elijah appreciated that as much as anything. It wasn't like talking to Preacher Ramey, who he'd run moonshine with when they were young men, or his lawyer Bane Wales, who ultimately just wanted as much of Elijah's money as he could finagle out of the old man through his legal fees and services. No, Josh listened and, when appropriate or requested, told Elijah what he thought, not just what Elijah wanted to hear.

Elijah snapped back to the present and looked up at the clock on the wall. Fifteen before noon, almost time for the local news out of Bluefield. He got up and crossed the little room to turn on the television. He went into the bathroom to relieve himself and wash up a little before he ate a bite of dinner. Josh and Agatha might be here directly, too, but Agatha had a doctor's appointment that morning, so he would just make his own dinner to show them that he was okay. It was mostly an act on his part. Elijah Miller was about as far from "okay" as a man could get, but he didn't want the kids and grandkids worrying about him unnecessarily.

Once he had cleaned up and fixed a couple of Treet meat sandwiches for himself, he poured a cup of coffee and went to sit in his swivel recliner a few feet from the color television set. The set was old and temperamental, which was probably why he wouldn't part with it – it was a lot like himself. Not much going on in the news. Kids gearing up for Halloween, more cold weather on its way, local politicians readying themselves for the elections just about a week or so away.... Then it would be time to make Thanksgiving preparations, then Christmas, and a new year. A new year without Reny in it. A new year with nothing really left to live for. A new year that Elijah hoped fervently would be his last.

He turned off the television set when the soaps came on. He didn't care nothing at all for them, although Reny had treated them characters like her own family. He couldn't help but smile a little, recalling how she would sit there and tell them what to do, what not to do, and laugh and cry with their successes and shortcomings. He couldn't help but wonder how his life might have been changed if he had let her love him even half that much. What might their life have been like if he just had not been so hell-bent on making her life as miserable as his own, for reasons that presented themselves long before they began courting? He shook his head and willed himself not to dwell on it, not to dwell on anything about Reny to save himself from realizing the sheer emptiness of his current existence.

He lay down on the bed after pulling the shades to drown out the late October sun-cloud mix. He never had slept well in broad daylight unless he was passed out drunk – which he hadn't been for almost 14 years now – and found himself more and more frequently drawing the shades to close out the world beyond the farmhouse that he now stayed inside of almost all the time. Sleep was typically not much kinder than his waking hours, as his mind seemed plagued with pictures and voices from the past, so many of which he truly preferred to forget completely, or at least not dwell on if he could help it.

He thought of that story by Charles Dickens about the miserly old man who gave nothing to nobody without expecting something in return, and even then not giving if he could help it. For most of his life, most folks had been just about afraid not to do what Elijah Miller wanted them to do. He was not necessarily an unkind or ungracious man, but a man with a sense for doing what he needed to do, regardless of who might get hurt in the process. He suspected that people either loved him or hated him, since he never left much middle ground for them to stand on. But he'd never lived to please others, just to do what he needed and wanted to get by and prosper as much as he could. He tried to be honest in business transactions, but he did believe in looking out for himself. And that had created more than a few enemies along the way.

Just like that Ebenezer Scrooge fellow, Elijah found himself being visited by haints more and more often. He didn't seem to be able to keep them away. It was as if every soul he had ever had trouble with insisted on coming to visit him now that Reny was gone. Like maybe they'd been waiting all these years for her to pass, so they wouldn't cause Elijah's moodiness and fear after their visits to be taken out on her.

And Reny came to him, too. Nearly every day, he saw her there in the old farmhouse, or heard her walking across the floors to get dinner fixed or to check on the fire in the cook stove. Sometimes he swore that he could smell her cornbread baking in the oven or see her sitting down on the back side of the bed to begin taking off her prosthetic leg – the result of him shooting her when completely soused in October 1934, when Reny was eight months pregnant with their fourth child. He would turn sometimes and catch just a glimpse of her looking over at him. Then she would be gone from sight, but never absent from his mind. He figured that she would talk to him eventually, but wondered what was keeping her from doing so now.

His mama, Nannie Lee, came calling as an apparition from time to time. Shortly before her death in August 1935, after Elijah had shot Reny almost a year earlier, Nannie Lee had actually shot him. His own mother had shot him, and with the heart-felt intention of killing him dead. He had come in drunk again and had upset the peace that usually existed without him being around and, for reasons she never could explain to him during those last weeks of her life, had taken a pistol and shot him while he slept. "Hate ain't the only reason to take up arms," she had whispered on her death bed.

Had it not been for one of the neighbors hearing the gunshot and the screaming of his young children upon seeing their daddy bleeding in his own bed, Elijah likely enough would have died. Lucky for Elijah, it was a neighbor he hadn't given any reasons to dislike him and the man loaded Elijah up on a horse-drawn sled he'd been hauling wood on that afternoon, and started to town with him. Someone in a car picked them up in Adria and took them the rest of the way to the doctor's home in time to save him. Even then, Elijah went back to drinking after his second haul of one year in the state penitentiary in Richmond, this time cut off with a governor's pardon – his childhood friend Bobby Fletcher just happened to be serving as the governor of the Commonwealth at that time.

That is really something, he thought to himself. *To be sentenced to imprisonment in the state penitentiary not once, but* twice, *and still only have to pull a total of about two to three years including waiting in the local jail to be taken to Richmond. And, even while in prison, having a fairly easy time of it because of my connections, my friends and acquaintances, folks I'd done favors for at some point or another. If I hadn't been so damned miserable for so long, I'd say I'm a lucky man!* He wondered ultimately if luck really had anything to do with it. More likely he could chalk it up to bribes, deals, and crooked politicians, and he wasn't sure that those factors could be counted in the column of "luck."

That first stint in prison was an eye-opener for Elijah. Even though he was only there for a year, he learned things that he would never forget. He saw inmates used and abused in unspeakable ways. Yet, they were all there for doing unspeakable things, so didn't they really deserve such mistreatment? He had been fortunate to be needed in the infirmary due to his knowledge of treating farm animals for various ailments. And serving his time in the infirmary was a sight better than being on a chain gang or other such service while imprisoned. He had certainly never complained about getting to help tend the sick or dying.

He had seen death come to many creatures in his life, some by his own hands, some by the hands of others, and some by the hands of God. Watching something die was certainly not the worst thing he could imagine. After all, killing Frankie Waldron was the reason he had ended up going to prison that first time. And he had watched Frankie die, too, a slower, less merciful death than Frankie had deserved at anyone's hands, much less those of his brother-in-law.

He fell off to sleep, but Frankie soon roused him up. "You'll never get shut of it, Elijah," the forever-young specter told him with an amused laugh. "You shot me down more than 50 years ago, but you will never, never, never forget how awful a thing it was to do to me! It has eaten away at you in your soberness, and even when you was drunk, Elijah. It has been ever-present, even in those moments when you thought for sure you were dying at your sweet mama's hands. You couldn't even ask God to forgive you in what might have been your dying moments because you could not get shook of what you done to me that Christmas night!"

Elijah tried to wake himself, but Frankie refused to let him go that easily this afternoon. "No, no, you never gave me a chance to speak my mind that night, Elijah. You never gave me a chance to try to convince you that you were mistaken in your allegations against me – to accuse me of cheating on your sister Beck with *anyone*, but especially with your sweet, young, innocent wife, Reny! The thing was, Lige, you knew that you didn't deserve Reny Collins – that girl was always gonna be too good for you! Her heart was purer than anything you'd ever stumbled upon in this world. But you was so blasted miserable with yourself that you had to try to pull everyone else down to the pits of hell with you! Reny wouldn't go down that road, though, would she? No, sir! She just kept believing and trusting in God, praying for your soul and for her life and for the lives of those four young'uns of yours. If you hadn't had the love of Reny, you'd have died long before now! That woman saved your life so many times! She forgave you of the despicable things that you did to her – to her face and behind her back!

"She forgave you for killing me, even though she knew you were wrong to do so, and she stood by you through the trial and waited until you got home from prison – and would have waited the other long years that you should have had to serve for murdering me in cold blood for absolutely no reason!

"She forgave you for shooting her in the leg while she was eight months pregnant with your youngest child, and even though she lost part of her leg to your pride, arrogance, and sheer callousness, she never once lost her hope that you would straighten up and be the man that she knew that you could be! She forgave you for not giving her stillborn child a proper burial on that hillside on Dry Fork so you didn't have to spend money on a coffin or a marker – she forgave you for beating her so hard that you caused her to lose that baby in the first place. She forgave you for all the hell that you put her through on every holiday when you decided that it was better to be drunk than risk being human around her and your children. She forgave you for lining up those four kids and shooting at them just to hear them scream, for trying to drown them in five-gallon buckets when you were drinking and didn't want to waste bullets on torturing them.

"She forgave you for sleeping with Oney Miller all those years, even the times you brought Oney here and made Reny sleep in the same bed with the two of you or you'd shoot her dead. She forgave you for introducing Oney as your wife in public while Reny sat at home waiting for you to come home so she could fix you a good meal and let you know how much she loved you!

"She forgave you for kicking out your son, your oldest child, just weeks after he came home from serving in the Korean War, because he had the audacity to stand up to you for beating Reny the way you did when things didn't go the way you wanted them to. She forgave you for never speaking to that son again before he died in that mine explosion over in Bishop just a few weeks after he left home and moved in with my own daughter's family because you said he was a bastard and not welcome in your home again.

"She forgave you for shooting her again, thirty years after the first time, and for threatening to kill both her and your youngest daughter if she dared to carry through with her intent to divorce you – because you might have to go to prison for the shooting, but you wouldn't stand to be made to look like a fool by being told in a court of law that you weren't worth her risking her life to be with you any longer!"

"STOP!" Elijah finally managed to scream, and shook himself awake from the horrible dream. He was cold with sweat and shaking all over. He hadn't cared for Frankie Waldron when he was living, and he was even less enthralled with him in death. Frankie spoke nothing but the truth, but he wouldn't let Elijah try to defend himself, to explain any of his reasons or irrationalities.

"And why should I let you try to explain?"

Elijah jumped up off the bed as he realized that Frankie was standing on the opposite side of the room from him, but that he himself was wide awake as this conversation continued. All he could see was a faint silhouette of Frankie in the room with the shades drawn. But he knew the voice. He knew the smell of Frankie's cologne, even all these years later. Every single memory of the man had haunted him his entire life, and each detail now seemed clearer than it had on the day he murdered Frankie. "Tell me, Elijah!" Frankie roared at him in such a way that Elijah could feel the floor vibrate beneath his feet. "I tried to explain things to you that Christmas night. I swore that I wasn't involved with Reny. I told you that your sister was the most important person in the world to me! I told you to leave that argument between Alley and me and that you shouldn't get involved, but you wouldn't listen to me at all!"

"I heard you," Elijah shouted back, but his voice sounded shrill and broken. "I heard every word you said that night, and I've heard them over and over and over again!"

"You might've heard 'em, Elijah, but you *never listened!* If you had listened to any part of it, you would not have pulled that trigger the first time to scare me, nor the second time to shoot me on behalf of Alley Mullins, who would never be man enough to confront me on his own, nor the third time for yourself on account of your inferiorities about losing the best thing that ever happened in your life, Reny Collins!"

"Okay, I'll admit it! I was wrong!" Elijah shook as he confessed this to the man he'd murdered more than 50 years ago.

Frankie Waldron's voice whooped in laughter. "Well, now, Elijah Miller, ain't that awfully big of you? You were wrong!" His laughter shook the house to the extent that Elijah saw the linoleum on the floor come up and roll across the floor like waves on a lake when disturbed by the wind. "You still ain't said that you were sorry!"

"Is that what you want?" Elijah jumped to his feet. "If I tell you that, will you go away and leave me alone forever?"

"Oh, Elijah, you ain't got forever, old boy! And just saying it don't mean a thing, not to me, not to you, not to nobody!"

At that moment, Elijah heard Aggie and Josh in the kitchen and he called out to them anxiously. "Aggie! Josh! Is that you?"

Frankie shook his head and chuckled. "This ain't over, Elijah. I promise you, it ain't near over!"

"The hell you say, Frankie, I'm done with you!" Elijah was saying as Josh stepped into the room.

Josh flipped on the light switch and looked around. "Elijah, who are you talking to?"

"Nobody, sonny, nobody," he mumbled and sat back down on the edge of the bed.

A couple of days went by with no further disturbances from the past. Maybe he was shut of Frankie and all of those horrible reminders of the things he had done wrong. No, he'd never be shut of it all, he knew that. Even if he never saw Frankie's face again, heard his voice, smelled his cologne, or felt his very presence three feet away from him again, he knew that he'd never stop thinking about the fact that Frankie was right and that he was wrong about every little bad thing he had tried to justify throughout his 72 years. He kept hearing Frankie's list of all the things that Reny had forgiven Elijah for. He supposed that he had managed to forget some of those things, or to put them so far back in the recesses of his mind that he could pretend he hadn't done them.

The days stretched into weeks, several of them. He had no further delusions about being free from reminders of his misdeeds, whether from the ghost of Frankie Waldron, or whether from his own addled mind. Christmas Day finally came and the family insisted on coming to the farmhouse to celebrate with him, even though he really wasn't doing much celebrating about anything at all these days. He did enjoy some time with his little great-granddaughter Adrian, though. She was in second grade and smart as a whip. And she had her Granddaddy wrapped around her little finger, which truthfully gave Elijah great pleasure to admit. He was even persuaded by Adrian to take out his banjo from its peg in his closet that no one was allowed into and play some of his favorite old tunes. She laughed and sang along to the ones she knew, and he thought to himself, *This is the one bright spot in my life!*

After everyone had left for the night, he shuffled through the house, again checking all of the doors to make certain that they were locked. He left on the kitchen light and the bathroom light. Despite the fact that he hated wasting money by leaving them on all night, he found them comforting in terms of keeping his ghosts at bay. He pulled the blinds and turned on the television, waiting for the eleven o'clock news.

And there he was. Frankie was back. He hadn't said a word yet, but Elijah knew that he was there. And he knew why he was there. There hadn't been a Christmas for more than 50 years that this particular memory hadn't come back to haunt Elijah. Elijah tried desperately to hold on to the happiness he had felt while playing with Adrian a short while ago, while playing his banjo and her singing along. Was it asking too much to hold on to that joy, to have one happy memory to replay in place of all of these other dastardly deeds?

"No, Elijah, that isn't asking too much," he heard Reny's voice softly whisper. "That Adrian is a true ray of sunshine, ain't she?"

He looked around, but couldn't see Reny. But he could hear her. Like she was sitting right beside him. And he believed that she was. He could almost feel her breath on his cheek. "I want the good times, Reny. Surely there were some good times, weren't there?"

"Elijah, there were some happy times, but you weren't really involved with most of them. You were so busy drinking, carousing, gambling, and trying to get ahead that you never just appreciated what was right there for you. And because of that, you've spent your whole life running from the things you've done. I told you before I passed on, I never loved no one like I love you."

"Like you love me," he repeated. "You still love me?"

"If I didn't still love you, I wouldn't be here, Elijah. I told Frankie that he had to give me a chance tonight before he lets in to you again. He's only doing what he has to do, Lige. This is his plight. You gave him no chance to make things right – not with you, not with Beck, not with God.

So he has to remind you of what you have done wrong in order to help you do what is right."

"I told him that he was right, that I was wrong, Reny," Elijah started.

"Elijah, hush up and listen," Reny's voice comforted and soothed him. "I went through hell on earth with you for more than 50 years of marriage. And I did that because I loved you. I knew what kind of man you could be, Elijah, if only you would let yourself be."

"I can't be that kind of man, Reny, you know the things I've done."

"That I do. But I also know that it isn't too late. Not yet. But it won't be too much longer, Elijah. You have amends to make, not just for your own sake, but for those who come after you. For Adrian," she added. "That little girl thinks there ain't no one like you. She and I talk about you sometimes."

"You – You talk to Adrian, too?" Elijah seemed surprised.

"I do. She knows that I will always be here for her. She needs to know that you will, too, even after you pass on. She isn't scared of us – those who've gone on, but come back as we watch over her. But she is innocent. No blood on her hands and no malice in her heart. Wouldn't you like for it to be that way for you, too, Elijah?"

He wanted to answer, to give her a resounding yes. But he knew that he deserved these constant reminders. He deserved this and much worse. "I can't, Reny. I just – I can't. I don't want it to be this way, but it is."

"Oh, Elijah," she patted his hand and he felt her do so and trembled and cried at her amazing touch. "I've already forgiven you. And Frankie, well, he *can't* forgive you – you didn't give him enough time to on the night that you killed him. The people from your past are from your past and you can't undo those things you've done, that's true. But you have got to make peace, once and for all – with those still here who want and need that from you. But mostly, you've got to answer to God and make it right with Him. I want you to come be with me and right now, you're not headed in that direction."

Elijah noticed for the first time since he'd felt Reny enter the room tonight that Frankie hadn't gone anywhere. His silhouette still lingered near the closet where Elijah's banjo hung. Reny's visit was a short reprieve from what waited for him when she left him. He closed his eyes and whispered through tears, "Reny, I loved you more than anything in the world. I just never knew how to show it – I never could figure out how to show you without losing myself in it all. I couldn't give myself away like that. I just never knew how."

"Then you best be figuring it out, Elijah," she spoke forthrightly and he felt her moving away from him.

He looked up, knowing that she was gone now. And Frankie started in on him once more.

(Old family picture of Elijah Vance, father of Jesse Abner Vance
– Jesse Vance being whom the character Elijah Miller is based
upon.)

Heart of the Matter:
A Difference-Maker in My Life

Many literary works make differences in people's lives, whether novels, plays, short stories, or poems. For me, lyrics (defined in Webster's New World Dictionary, 3rd College Edition, as "poetry or a poem mainly expressing the poet's emotions and feelings") have always spoken in a deeper way than just hearing a song on the radio. The best lyrics tell a story or share a truth about life in such a way that hearing the lyrics within the context of the song makes meaning of both words and melody. One of the first sets of lyrics to resonate with me in this way was written by Don Henley, Mike Campbell, and J.D. Souther, and is entitled, "Heart of the Matter." This particular set of lyrics helped me to realize that one of life's greatest gifts to give or receive is forgiveness.

My mother and father separated when I was six months old. During my childhood and my teenage years, my father did little to be part of my life, including paying court-mandated child support. For several of those years, my mother raised me as a single parent. To say that she harbored ill feelings toward my father and his lack of accepting responsibility is an understatement. I did not realize until my early 20's, however, though, how much Mom's feelings about my father were showing up in my own choices and attitudes towards men in general, and specifically, towards my estranged father. At the age of 23, I heard "Heart of the Matter" one night and jotted down the lyrics to one part in particular.

> There are people in your life who've come and gone
> They let you down and hurt your pride
> You've gotta put it all behind you; life goes on
> You keep carryin' that anger, it'll eat you up inside....
> I've been tryin' to get down to the Heart of the Matter
> Because the flesh will get weak
> And the ashes will scatter
> So I'm thinkin' about forgiveness
> Forgiveness
> Even if, even if you don't love me anymore.

It was the first time in my life that I realized how frequently I pushed guys away when I felt like I was getting too close. There was a definite fear of abandonment, but also an unhealthy sentiment of "you remind me of my father, so I will throw you away before you get the chance to do that to me." And the truly ironic part of the situation existed in the fact that I knew almost nothing about my father. I knew only the barest of factual data – date of birth, the county where he was born, his parents' names, that he was one of twelve children, but little else except the bitter stories on which I was raised.

Knowing how little I knew about my father bothered me; it actually haunted me. Even if *he* could live without knowing or caring about whom I was or anything else about me, I decided that I was not approaching his life that way any longer. Henley's words stuck with me: "You keep carryin' that anger, it'll eat you up inside." For my entire life, that had happened. I had fed off of my mother's anger and bitterness and had claimed it as my own. But I made a conscious decision, refusing to let it affect *me* when it did nothing to *him*. I would not live my life that way any longer. The result was a phone call a few months later and more than a decade of my father and me getting to know each other better. The relationship is far from perfect; but the important part to me is that I forgave him.

I forgave him for abandoning us – for making my life such a struggle growing up. I also came to accept that, as difficult as I thought my life was without him, it likely would have been far more challenging with an alcohol-abusing father. In addition to forgiving him, I forgave my mother for how she taught me to feel about my father; I do not blame her for her feelings, but her feelings cannot sustain me. I forgave myself for letting things that happened when I was too young to even form an opinion keep me from getting to know an entire side of my family until I had grown to adulthood, to lose so many years of living and loving people who wondered about me and would have welcomed me with open arms. I learned that forgiveness comes in all sizes and is useful for just about any occasion. Sometimes it just takes getting down to the "Heart of the Matter" to find it.

Diner Dude

It was my second trip to Chattanooga in two weeks, a second conference in that same span of time. The first week, I had been on-hand for the Celebration of Southern Literature, a three-day event doing just what it proclaimed, and this second week, I was in town for the annual Tennessee Library Association Conference, my first in about seven years.

I crossed the street to the City Café Diner. It was a modest establishment on the corner of Martin Luther King and Carter Street, with a sign proudly announcing that it was open 24 hours a day. Not the sort of place I typically enjoy, to be quite honest. I stopped hanging out in places like that when I was in college. After spending so many nights with inebriated friends trying to sober up in hole-in-the-wall diners back in those days, I grew weary of such establishments and simply quit going to them. I enjoyed the occasional Shoney's, but nothing that stayed open 24 hours a day; those were scary places – those were haunts for the deluded and drunken souls of the world and I was beyond that. Yet this place had seemed so different last week. I probably chalked it up to the foot-long four-inch-wide éclairs and eight-inch-high cheesecakes in their dessert counters. Seriously, how could a place with desserts like that be bad?

Upon entering, I waited beside the sign that instructed me to do so before being seated, and a gentleman in a white dress shirt and tie asked if I'd like a table. "Yes, please, for one," I answered casually, remembering a time when announcing that I would be dining alone would have smothered me in embarrassment and/or sadness. He eyed me oddly, and then took me to a booth in the back, literally hidden from view of anything from the front of the diner. I ordered an unsweetened tea with lots of lemon, picked up the menu, and pondered whether a 24-hour diner's "Tour of Milan" could possibly measure up to Olive Garden's "Tour of Italy." Surely ordering such from the menu would just turn out to be a travesty....

A young couple entered and was seated in the booth in front of me. I couldn't help but listen to them. His accent sounded like that of a young man I'd had quite the crush on in my own college days, the things he said reminding me of the same young man. The girl sat there mostly quietly, as though listening to him in all of his grandeur, the exquisite way he had his whole life planned out, the self-assured tone of everything he said, the way he talked about all of the ready-made contacts that his parents had for him, especially his businessman father.... I felt like I had been transported back in time half of my lifetime ago.

When Barbie and Ken left, the table sat empty for a while and I chewed my chicken sandwich slowly, wondering if I would sell any books in the next three days, wondering if the investment of coming back to Chattanooga would pay off. I had been besieged with an allergy headache, sniffles, and sore throat during my stay the first week, and had managed to get in to see my doctor at home during that one-day window before coming back. In truth, I did not feel completely well and the thoughts of a long night of sleep had begun to lure me out of the booth and back to the parking garage just when a disheveled man slid into the Barbie and Ken's booth alone, onto the bench side facing me and began murmuring under his breath, "I like you; I like you a lot."

I looked around slowly, convinced that the allergy medication had made me loopier than I realized, but there was no one else in our vicinity. The man was wearing a navy blue sweat suit, despite the fact it had to be every bit of 80 degrees outside. His hair was dark black with a Mohawk down the middle of shorter-cropped hair to the sides. Dark brown eyes pierced me for the split-second that I met his gaze. I went back to pretending to look at something important on my iPod.

Just then, our server came back to greet him. "Hi, my name is Lisa, I'll be your server this evening. What would you like to drink?"

He looked up at her as if she had just spoken to him in a foreign language of some sort. "What did you say your name is?"

"Lisa," the server repeated. "What would you like to drink?"

"I'd like some orange juice. And ice water." Lisa nodded and walked away, eyeing him suspiciously. The man continued in a hushed tone, as if she were still standing there. "But don't mix them together. Not like the last time. Or I'll have to throw them against the wall again!"

I kept looking at my iPod, posting my position and what was happening to my friends on Facebook. Suddenly, I'd realized I was in this back corner with no way out except to walk past him. And I honestly didn't feel safe doing so. Maybe it was the way he kept picking up the knife from his cutlery and rubbing it along the palm of his hand. Maybe it was the way he kept murmuring to himself. Or maybe it was because he looked up at me suddenly and said, "Wanna hear a funny story? I've got a bunch of 'em!" He caught me looking at him as he did so, but I quickly looked back down at the iPod and posted more of the unfolding scenario on Facebook.

Diner Dude flipped through the menu for what seemed like forever, apparently torn between two dishes. Aloud, he pondered (or maybe asked me, I'm still not certain), "Do I want an omelet, or do I want the burrito?" He repeated over and over, "Omelet? Burrito? Omelet? Burrito?" So many times that I almost laughed out loud.

My Facebook friends were throwing out varying suggestions from "Just enjoy the bit of crazy" to "AWE-

SOME" to "You owe it to yourself to write a story about this to share at the next Night Writers Guild meeting!" I kinda snickered and agreed; it would make a cool story. I wasn't quite sure about what, but hey, writers can fill in the blanks about that stuff; it's what we do, right?

Lisa eventually came back as far as his table (not to mine) with his water and orange juice and put them down at arm's length from her, obviously not wanting to get too close to the man. I wondered if he smelled bad up close; I remembered the incredible stench present on some of the people who frequented the public library I'd first worked in when I moved to Bristol more than a decade before. I couldn't detect anything like that from Diner Dude from where I sat, but maybe you had to be closer, I thought. "What do you want to eat?" she asked him in a huff.

He looked at the menu again, then up at her. He looked pensive, as though this was a matter that he took incredibly seriously. Then he asked with a smile, "I'm sorry. I forgot your name again."

Visibly frustrated, Lisa shook her head and exhaled, blowing her bangs upward as she did so. "LISA!" she practically shouted at him. "My name is LISA!"

He seemed taken aback, as anyone would have. "I'm sorry, Lisa. Sometimes I just have a problem remembering things. My memory doesn't work as well as it used to. Not like it did before I went to Iraq."

She shook her head and interrupted him. "Look, do you know what you want to eat, or not?"

He pursed his lips and asked, "Which is better? The omelet, or the burrito?"

"Look, mister! I have no clue what you like or what you want. Just pick one and order already, okay?"

He cocked his head a little to the right and apologized. "Have I done something to make you mad?"

She shifted her weight to her other foot and tried to ease up on the man a little. "I'm just really, really busy, mister. And the more time I spend over here, the less I'm making in tips somewhere else, okay?"

He nodded, seemingly understanding the implication of her words. "Well, then, I guess I'll have the omelet. With bacon and mushrooms and jalapenos. And toast on the side." She started to walk away, but he reached out and touched her arm to stop her. His voice was again hushed and sounded rough and forceful. "No strawberry jelly, though, or I will throw it against the wall and make a bigger mess than you've ever seen in your life!"

She looked at him in either fear or disgust, maybe a mixture of the two, and walked away again, shaking her head and making a sign to her manager to indicate that she was dealing with someone who was obviously not stable.

I made sure I was once again intently absorbed in the iPod when she left, but heard Diner Dude talking and looked up just enough to realize that he was talking to me.

"I don't know where you come from, but I'll figure it out. Oh, yes, I will figure it out."

What did he mean? Part of me wanted to talk to him, to ask what in the world he was talking about, but as I continued to type in what was going on into Facebook, more people were advising me to "Run, run, run!" One friend said, "My advice is to get up, pick up your purse, and SLOWLY walk toward the 'bathroom.' Then go out the nearest exit, get in your SUV, and go somewhere else to eat." I explained that I couldn't do that. I had to see this thing through. There was a story here and I needed to know more of it. The same friend proceeded to call me a "big dingo," and accuse me of being willing to take my life into my own hands for the sake of a story.

For not the first time in my life, I wondered if she wasn't correct on this point. How smart was it to continue to sit here and observe this man who couldn't be entirely sane for the sake of a good story? He had been talking to himself – or to someone invisible to the rest of us – since he arrived in the restaurant. He had threatened the server at least twice with throwing things against the wall. He had spoken to me in riddles that perplexed, confused, but somehow also intrigued me. Then I envisioned a horrific massacre, ripped straight from the headlines of the 11 o'clock news and wished I had someone there with me, maybe a handsome man who would protect me if Diner Dude did get out of hand…

About that time, Diner Dude pointed beside me, to the empty space I'd just been wishing was occupied by a handsome man. "I don't care who your boyfriend there beside you is, I like you anyway."

I couldn't help but look beside me at the empty seat. How had he done that? Was he a mind-reader in addition to be being crazy? *Oh, Lord! I better be careful what I think! I don't wanna piss him off!*

Diner Dude went on, talking to me quietly, but loudly enough for me to clearly hear what he was saying. "You make me smile, you make me happy. So I'm not afraid of him. There!" He laughed, making the hair on my arms stand on end. "And I like your freakin' t-shirt, too, whoever the hell that is on it!" I looked down at my Bon Jovi t-shirt and swallowed hard, wondering if I should have worn my newest Duran Duran t-shirt with no faces on it instead of this one.

He laughed again, louder this time. "I should have ordered the burrito," he commented. "Yeah, you're hot and spicy, like a burrito. I should have ordered the burrito. I should have ordered the damned burrito!" and with that, he slammed the knife down onto the table angrily and shouted, "Where the hell is my food? How long does it take to get an order around here?"

Only no one was listening to him. I heard him. I knew he had just shouted. I knew that he had just had an outburst in public. Yet no one paid any attention. Not even me, really. I kept my eyes on the iPod and entered more text on Facebook, at this point, thinking it might be the last stuff anyone ever heard from me.

A few minutes later, a cook from the back brought out his omelet and sat it down without asking if there was anything else that he needed. He walked away disinterested. Diner Dude looked around and suddenly called out, "Where is my toast? I ordered toast, for God's sake!"

Lisa appeared and sat down the toast, reaching carefully across the table and removing the strawberry jelly from the jelly holder that sat on the table. "Here. Take your damned toast!" she said to him. "I forgot it." Then she added. "I think I got all of the strawberry jelly out of there. But just in case I missed one, please don't smear it all over the wall! I really don't feel like cleaning up a mess tonight!"

He nodded politely and thanked her for her attention and service, like a totally different person, and began to eat like he hadn't eaten in days. I couldn't help but watch and wonder more about who he was and what his story truly was. The music in the background was all 80s stuff, pleasing to my ears and soul. An old favorite by Crowded House came on. "Don't Dream It's Over." I smiled, thinking of an old college friend who used to sing it with me.

"I'll sing this song to you," Diner Dude announced sweetly, and I actually looked up without meaning to. "But I'll stab you with this fork first!" he grimaced at me and slammed his fork down, tines-end first onto the Formica surface of the table.

I can't exactly explain why, but I didn't look away. It was like I knew that doing so would show that I was afraid of him, which, in that moment, I was. Very much so. But I refused to admit that to him. Unless he really *could* read my mind, in which case I had just done so. He smiled again and went back to eating his omelet and toast with grape jelly. So I went back to updating my Facebook status.

I wished that Lisa would come back so I could order some dessert to go or get my bill or another unsweetened tea. Something. But I had a gut feeling that Lisa, much like Elvis, had left the building. And I was stuck. As another friend remarked on Facebook, "So you missed your chance to leave safely, basically."

Yes. I had missed my chance to leave safely. I had been drawn in to a train wreck and couldn't leave. Now I was just hoping that the eventual derailment didn't take me out as well. Why was I drawn to people and situations like this? Why was I willing to play on the edge of danger like this for the sake of a good story and an interesting character? Didn't that make me at least as crazy as the people I was writing about?

Someone at the cash register started complaining about the cost of insurance and the sad state of affairs in America. I braced myself. I'm not sure how or why, but I knew that a fuse had just been lit and that explosives would soon go off at the booth across from me.

"Hey, I'll tell you what the problem is," Diner Dude called as he wiped his mouth and stood up, leaving his plate of mostly-eaten food to approach the counter. "The problem is that nobody gives a damn anymore! That's what the problem is! Nobody cares. And when nobody cares, what the hell else do you think is gonna happen? You can't expect nothing good to happen when people don't care no more than they do! And then there's all the politicians in DC and none of them care, either. Not about nobody but themselves! They don't care about nobody that went to war or came back all messed up or whatever..."

The manager looked at Diner Dude and spoke sharply, "Hey, look, you don't need to talk like that in here, mister! Why don't you just get your stuff together and get out of here?"

My mouth dropped open. It was probably the most lucid line of verbiage Diner Dude had spoken since he'd entered the place and he was being reprimanded for it. He hadn't threatened anyone. He hadn't even been rude, really. He had spoken what probably couldn't have been more fervent truth from anyone, anywhere. And he was being kicked out.

He retaliated. "Oh, sure! I see how you're going to be! I speak against the establishment and you're gonna throw me out!" He threw back his head and laughed maniacally. "Oh, that's rich, absolutely rich!"

I wondered if he had staged the outburst at this point to get out of paying for his dinner. Not a stupid move for a homeless man, I decided, just as he marched back up to the counter and demanded his check. "I will not leave until I get my check. I won't walk out on a bill! I'm not part of the problem here, you know!"

I watched, wide-eyed and bewildered. Where had this lucidity been the rest of the night? And then, just as quickly as it had all appeared, it seemed to be gone. As the manager handed him the check, Diner Dude proclaimed, "My mother's waited tables here for thirty years and you know what?" Without waiting enough time for anyone to give voice to an answer, he continued. "I'm her son! I'm her son, dammit! And now you're gonna throw me out?!?!?" He shook his head and came back to the booth to sit down, the manager walking towards him and everyone in the diner watching him nervously. Except me. I looked at the iPod and typed as if my life depended on it. Maybe somehow it did.

"Look, mister, I don't need you in here throwing a fit —"

Diner Dude shouted back, defending himself from something, but I'm not sure if even he knew what. "We ain't throwing nothing! This ain't Alabama!" And with that, he sighed in frustration and began counting out a handful of coins from his baggy sweatpants pocket.

He looked over at me once more as he started another pile of coins, presumably for Lisa's tip. "Thirty years my mother's waited tables here. Thirty years. *My mother.* And I am her son! *Her son!* These people don't have a clue!" The manager pointed to the door and waited for Diner Dude to move towards it.

"Not a clue," he said, looking at me once more before leaving under his own power, with his self-respect intact, if not his entire mental faculties.

(Photo by Chrissie Anderson Peters, at Late Bar, Chicago, IL, 20 October 2013)

The "Me" in Team

At the end of ninth grade, Sparky Johnson wrote in my yearbook, "I'd tell you to have a fun summer, but I'm sure you'll just be reading or something." It incensed me to no end! As if there was nothing more to me than reading! As if I, Cassandra Lansing, could not be fun! I took it personally and spent the whole summer trying to figure out some way of changing my image (between reading books, of course). I used Sun-In every time I went to the pool and was a bleach-blonde by the time I got back to Springmont High for my sophomore year. That alone probably would not have done it, but I figured it was a good first step in the right direction. After all, weren't blondes supposed to have more fun?

In our traditional assembly on the first day of school, I sat with my best friends, Rebecca and Shelly. We chitchatted while we should have been listening, just like everyone else, while tired-looking homeroom teachers patrolled the auditorium.

Suddenly, Dr. Foster, the principal, was saying something about the junior varsity girls' basketball team needing more players in order to be eligible to have a team. "They only have three members," I heard him say as I shushed Rebecca and Shelly, to make sure I didn't miss something important.

I didn't know much about basketball. I didn't know much about any sport, to be completely honest. I had always been overweight. Add to that the fact that I was asthmatic. And I wore make-up at all times. Did I mention that I hated my knees because God put them on backwards and that basketball shorts of the late 80's were short enough to show that to the whole world?

Still, I knew that there had to be at least *five* people or there could not be a team. The first game was in two nights. I sat there smiling, seeing a childhood dream about to come true on some level. I remembered watching the Harlem Globetrotters cartoon in elementary school and going outside with a regular red rubber ball because I didn't have a basketball and we couldn't afford one. I'd pretend to do cool tricks with my ball, although I could only dribble it and that was about the extent of my talent. Here was my chance. I reasoned that they couldn't cut me from the team – they had to have at least two more people to even have a team, and surely they would want a few extra people in case anyone got into foul trouble (whatever that meant, exactly). I was smart – I could learn to do anything if there was someone willing to teach me. Look out, Sparky Johnson! A new Cassandra Lansing was on her way!

Coach Beth Hoops – hand-to-God that was the JV coach's name – looked at me and at the other seven girls who had showed up for that first practice. "Dear God," she muttered. "What the hell am I supposed to do with this crew?" She looked at my physical form. "You have asthma and you want to play basketball?"

"I'm fine as long as I don't run a lot."

She looked at me, incredulous at my lack of knowledge of the game. "Lansing, have you ever played basketball?"

"No, m'am."

"Then why do you want to play?"

I had thought out this part carefully. I'd already had to convince my mother, who was certain I would quit halfway through the season. "I want to be part of a team, part of something bigger than just me. I want to learn how to play and how to rely on others, how to help and be helped. Everything I've ever done has just been me figuring out how to do things on my own." I could see that she wasn't swayed, so I added, "Plus, I know that you have to have at least five bodies in order to have a team. I can help you have at least five bodies."

She twisted up her mouth, somewhere between a frown and a look of "Well, you've got me there." She told me to take my place on the bench with the others. I knew most of the other girls in name, if not personally. The point-guard was a friend of mine, Toni. She smiled and waved from her seat way up the line. I sat in the eighth chair in line. The last seat on the bench.

I learned lots in the weeks to come. I learned that I loathed practices. I learned that I had so little natural athleticism that I was nigh-on pathetic. I learned that basketball is 99.9% running and that I better keep my asthma inhaler close-by at all times. I also learned that, if I did anything to make Coach Hoops unhappy, her preferred punishment for me was to make me run more laps – thus, more suckage off the inhaler. In short, I learned that I really could not do anything to make Coach happy. I don't think that anyone else could, either, but it especially disheartened me.

After our first game (which we lost, of course), Coach Hoops made us join hands in the locker room. "All right now, we're gonna pray, dammit!" And she led us in the Lord's Prayer. I couldn't help but look around. Was anyone else waiting for God to strike us all down because she started us out by swearing? At least half of us were "praying" with bowed heads, but open eyes, although Coach seemed fervent in her supplication to God. I couldn't decide whether to laugh or be scared. After Coach left the locker room, we all let out giggles of confusion and relief, one person adding that that had been the weirdest prayer she'd ever prayed. But every post-game prayer had gone much the same way, whether we won or lost.

One evening at practice, I thought that I might *finally* be getting somewhere, that Coach might *finally* be changing her mind about me. I felt my spirits lighten, thinking, "*Finally*! She is giving me the benefit of the doubt!"

"Lansing," she said in her gruff tone. "You remind me exactly of myself when I was in high school." She continued, with barely a beat skipped, "I hated myself in high school."

For the most part, I spent the season dressed out in that hideous uniform, just sitting on the bench. If I got to play at all, Coach Hoops would stick me in for the final 10-20 seconds of the game. And that was only if we were winning so strongly or losing so badly that there was no chance of things turning around. I hated everything about the game. I hated everything about the practices. If I started to catch myself smiling about something, maybe a joke that Coach had cracked or something, I'd quickly throw up the walls again. After all, if she was going to hate me, I figured I would just return the favor. Either way, I realized, I was going to be miserable, which I figured was her full intent.

By mid-season, I wanted to quit so badly, but I couldn't because my mother had foretold that I would. So, the entire second half of the season, I was doing mental battle against both Coach Hoops and my mother – because one devil wasn't bad enough!

One night, in a game against an eighth grade team, we were drilling them by halftime, up by more than forty points when we went into the locker room. My friend Toni, the point-guard and star player of our team, approached Coach Hoops in a whispered conversation and Coach emphatically retorted, "No!"

When we got back out to the floor, Toni refused to go back in the game. "My stomach hurts," she said as she looked down at her fingernails.

Our lead shrank to thirty points, and then twenty. Toni still wouldn't go in. Finally, with a look of sheer disgust, Coach said to Toni, "Fine, I'll put her in! You get your butt back in there!" Coach looked down the bench at me and pointed for me to go in. As I did so, Toni jumped up and followed me. I got fouled. I missed my first foul shot. As I focused for that second shot, I realized what Toni had done, how much she had put on the line for me to have a real chance to play in a game. And I missed the second foul shot, too. Damn! Toni came over, patted me on the back and said, "Great try, Cass, great try!"

The last week of practices, I had come down with a nasty case of bronchitis. Up to this point, I had not missed a single practice. I had missed plenty of Wednesday night church services, a huge no-no in my faith, but no basketball practices at all. My doctor forbade me to do any running. I still dressed out for the practices, though. I retrieved balls, did ball drills, anything that I could get by with that wasn't running. Because, by now, I understood what being part of a team was all about. I had become friends with these other seven girls. I cared about how they did on tests, how things were at home, how their romantic relationships were going, things I would never have even considered four months before.

The last home game of the season was a pretty big deal. Each player came out of the locker room, stopped center court, and was announced individually, while everyone stood and cheered. I was actually excited about this prospect. Even though I was only a bench warmer, my image had actually changed some during that first semester of sophomore year, and I had no doubt that it was thanks to my involvement with the basketball team.

I came into the locker room after going out to McDonald's with some of the other girls to grab a bite before the game. Coach Hoops stopped me as I reached into my duffle bag to get my uniform. "Lansing, you're not dressing out tonight. Since you've got that doctor's excuse, I really can't let you dress for the game." She went on to add. "In fact, you don't even have to sit on the bench, if you don't want to."

I stopped and looked at her, dumbfounded. I had dressed for every practice that week. I had still participated as fully as possible. And now she was taking this last game from me. She was refusing to let me dress, refusing to let me be acknowledged publically as an individual who had helped make up this team from day one of the season. I felt like I'd been smacked across the face.

My teammates stopped what they were doing – dressing, eating, whatever. They looked from Coach to me and back to Coach. Toni spoke first. "I guess none of the rest of us needs to sit on the bench if we don't want to, either, then. If Cass isn't going to be recognized as a member of this team for everything that she has done this season, then none of the rest of us needs to bother, either." And she picked up her bag and started to walk out of the locker room. Immediately, three other girls picked up their bags.

Coach Hoops stuttered and then announced, "Well, what am I supposed to do? I can't let her dress for the game."

Toni retorted, "You let her dress for practices all week! Let her dress. She just can't play. It won't be that different from how you've treated her all season!" Other girls nodded and concurred.

Coach looked from them to me and relented, realizing, I suppose, that Toni had a point.

I hugged Toni. And my other teammates huddled around me and we all cheered each other on, knowing we had already won tonight.

John Daniel Hash: Reconstructing a Life

(Family Photo of John Daniel Hash and "second" wife Cora Alberta "Bertie" Davis Hash)

I began researching my family history in April 2005 when two of my mother's first cousins from Maryland came to visit the family in Tazewell, Virginia and to search the courthouse for family information. As a librarian (and because my mama said so), it fell to me to show them around and help them navigate the collections at the public library and at the courthouse. I had interacted with genealogists for over a decade professionally and had no interest in becoming one myself. I have always thrived on family stories, but never had much use for recording them in any way. During our research quests that April day, it suddenly occurred to me that someone had to find this information and keep it down for posterity; and apparently, it was going to be me.

WHERE TO BEGIN?

No one had ever taught me how to "do" genealogical research. But it made sense to me to start with what I knew. Since I was researching in Tazewell, I decided it would make sense to look for my mother's maternal grandparents, Jesse Abner Vance and Daisy Irene Hash Vance. I hit a brick wall with my great-grandfather's great-grandfather, (great-great-great-great-grandfather), but I wanted to keep researching. So I turned my attention to Granny's family, the Hashes. So far as I knew, the Hashes were from the Tazewell area; Mamaw knew next-to-nothing about their origins. Her youngest sister Betty had done a lot of genealogy work before she died in 2000, but it had never interested anyone else in the family to any extent.

It wasn't much, but I did have Granny and Granddaddy Vance's birth dates and death dates. I was fortunate enough to actually know my great-grandparents and spent much of my pre-school childhood with them at their farmhouse in the Baptist Valley section of Tazewell. Granny died in May 1978, when I was in first grade;

Granddaddy died in January 1979, when I was in second grade.

The first document that I found regarding their life together was their marriage license, discovered in a drawer at the Tazewell County Courthouse.[1] This document records Daisy Hash's parents as John Hash and Bertie Hash, identifies the mailing address of both the bride and groom as Adria, Virginia (another community in Tazewell), and notes that the couple was married at "the bride's home." It gives the marriage date as 29 November 1926 and lists the groom's age as 20 and the bride's as 18 (which is incorrect, as Daisy was born in July 1910).[2]

Next I set about looking for a marriage license at the Tazewell County Court House for John and Bertie. According to the document on file there, John Hash (no middle name or initial listed) married Cora A. Davis on 3 March 1902.[3] My grandmother verified that Bertie's full name was Cora Alberta and that she was a Davis before marrying John Daniel Hash. The couple was married at "the Home of the Bride['s] Mother." Both the bride and

[1] Marriage license and certificate for Jesse Vance and Daisy Hash, Tazewell County Clerk's Office, Tazewell, Virginia.

[2] Interview with Dorothy Irene Vance Little (160 Little Acres Rd., N. Tazewell, VA 24630), by Chrissie Anderson Peters, 20 April 2005. [Mrs. Little, my maternal grandmother, has this information in the family Bible at her home.]

[3] Marriage license and certificate for John Hash and Cora A. Davis], Tazewell County Clerk's Office, Tazewell, Virginia.

the groom are recorded as having been born in Grayson County, Virginia, John being 22 years of age and Bertie being 16. John's parents are listed as "John & Elizabeth Hash" and Bertie's are given as "Monroe & Mary Davis." Both the groom and the bride are shown as "single," given the options of "widowed or single or divorced." Presuming that all of this information was correct, John Daniel Hash would have been born about 1880 and Bertie would have been born about 1886. Armed with the new-found knowledge that both of them were supposedly born in Grayson County, I turned to the Internet and began searching for any "John Hash" and/or "Elizabeth Hash" that I could find in that county around 1880.

JOHN HASH OF GRAYSON COUNTY

I found more John Hashes than I could keep straight! All of them seemed to go back to a fellow known as "Old John Hash," and "Old John Hash" was married twice, and had apparently deemed it necessary to have a son named John by each of his wives (identified in his Last Will and Testament as "John by my first wife and John by my second").[4] This gave way to more and more descendants of the same name, making the tracking process of my great-great-grandfather John Daniel Hash a task that I was truly not prepared for.

[4]Hash, Lee. "OJH" post on RootsWeb: HASH-L on 30 January 2005. Online at http://archiver.rootsweb.ancestry.com/th/read/HASH/2005-01/1107139700 Accessed 8 September 2011.

Thankfully, I came across a website called "New River Notes" (hereafter referred to as NRN) (www.NewRiverNotes.com). I found a transcription of the 1880 Grayson County census for the Wilson District.[5] The surname "Hash" appeared there 50 times. There appeared the following John Hashes: 1) John Hash, age 47, married to Rosa, age 45, no sons named John listed; and 2) John A. Hash, age 23, married to Sarah C. Hash, age 20, no children listed. Neither seemed to be the correct John Hash, as there was no wife named Elizabeth in either circumstance.

Through the NRN email discussion list, I quickly discovered a plethora of family connections (not only through the Hashes, but also through my father's family lines of Anderson and Parks, and Blevinses and Osbornes related to my mother's father who was born in Ashe County, North Carolina). Unfortunately for me, however, no one seemed to know anything about a John Daniel Hash. It was suggested that I check the Ashe County, North Carolina census records, since several of the Hashes lived in that neighboring county, as well. Another website yielded an index of all of the names included on that census, and this list indicated that there were John Hashes listed on pages 83, 87, and 88 – and that there was also an Elizabeth listed on page 87.[6] I accessed the 1880 Ashe

---

[5] Weaver, Jeffrey C., transcriber. "1880 Federal Census for Wilson District, Grayson County, Virginia." http://newrivernotes.com/va/wilson80.htm Accessed 27 August 2011.

County census through HeritageQuest at my local public library. That 1880 Ashe County census led me to the correct John Hash, father of my great-great-grandfather, John Daniel Hash. This "correct" John Hash was 66 years old as of that census and the family resided in the Chestnut Hill section of Ashe County; Elizabeth, his wife, was 36 years old. Children residing at home included Franklin (son, age 17), Fields (son, age 16), Lee (son, age 13), Creed (son, age 12), Alace (daughter, age 11), Ahort (son, age 6), Thomas (son, age 4), and John (son, age 1). Also living in the home was Elizabeth Hawks, who was listed as the head of household's mother (but was actually his mother-in-law), age 89, widowed. All of the children except Fields are listed as being born in North Carolina; Fields is listed as being born in Virginia. John, the father, is shown as born in Virginia, as was his father; his mother is shown as born in North Carolina. Elizabeth, the mother, is also shown as born in Virginia, with her father's birth state as "unknown," and her mother's as North Carolina.[7]

Eventually, Jeff Weaver, then moderator of the New River Notes website, cousin many times over, and

---

[6] "Index to 1880 Ashe County, NC Census: H." http://jctcuzins.org/census/ashe_h.html Accessed 24 August 2011.

[7] 1880 U.S. Federal Census (Population Schedule), Chestnut Hill Township, Ashe, NC, Page 30, Line 40, John Hash household, jpeg image, (Online: ProQuest Company, 2009) [Digital scan of original records in the National Archives, Washington, DC], subscription database, <http://www.heritagequestonline.com/>, accessed 31 July 2010.

renowned historian and all-around "regional" expert, shared with me the story of John and Elizabeth's tragic death – the couple froze to death in early February in either 1892[8] or 1895.[9] Once I had identified John Daniel's father as John Hawkins Hash, several researchers were able to provide me with John Hawkins Hash's lineage back to "Old John Hash." John Hash who was married to Elizabeth Hawks was known as John Hawkins Hash (although I have never seen any documentation showing this middle name or even an initial for him); his father was Robert "Bobby" Hash, who was married to Margery Hart; Robert's father was William Horton Hash (again, to my knowledge, no documentation exists identifying a middle name or initial for William Horton Hash), who was married to Ellender Osborne; it is generally accepted that William Horton Hash was a son of "Old John Hash" through his first marriage, therefore likely being the oldest son to move into the New River area from the Shenandoah region of Virginia with his father.[10] I had my lineage, but I still knew almost nothing about my great-great-grandfather. Who was John Daniel Hash and how did he get from the Grayson/Ashe area to Tazewell County?

---

[8] Email correspondence with Jeff Weaver from 8 October 2005.

[9] Email correspondence with Lee Hash from 12 October 2005.

[10] Email correspondence with Bette Nelson from 6 July 2005.

TRYING TO ASCERTAIN A YEAR OF DEATH

Assuming that 1879 is an accurate year for John Daniel Hash's birth, he would not have been an adult when his parents froze to death together, but would have been approximately 13 if they died in 1892 or 16 if they died in 1895. Questions abounded! Was he with them when they died? If not, where was he? If so, how did he survive when they did not?

I can only speculate on these points and have no real evidence for any of my suspicions. No local newspapers exist in archives that might have recorded the story of the tragic death of this couple.[11] No family stories seem to include any of the children being at home when the parents died.

The death date on the footstones of the couple is recorded as 6 February 1892[12]; I have seen this date in person on many occasions. It is my understanding through correspondence with Jeff Weaver that this date was firmly given by Hurdle Hash, a grandson of John and Elizabeth (his father was their son Lee Hash) who saw to the maintenance of the Elisha Anderson Cemetery where the couple is buried in the Grassy Creek community of Ashe

[11] Email correspondence with Jeff Weaver from 18 November 2005.

[12] New River Notes Photo Gallery. Headstone/Footstones of John Hawkins Hash and Elizabeth Hawks Hash in the Elisha Anderson Cemetery in Ashe County, North Carolina. http://photos.newrivernotes.com/displayimage.php?album=search&cat=0&pos=3 Accessed 12 September 2011.

County, until his own death in 1997. [13] [14] Lee Hash of Culpeper, Virginia (a descendant of John Hawkins Hash's sister Sarah Hash and her husband/cousin John Hash – not to be confused with Hurdle Hash's father Lee Hash mentioned above, who was a son of John and Elizabeth), is another Hash researcher who has aided in my quest for clues and answers with this family. He has supplied the year of John and Elizabeth's death as 1895, his information coming through another descendant of John and Elizabeth who lived near their resting place in the Elisha Anderson Cemetery in the Grassy Springs community of Ashe County, North Carolina.

Armed with the two potential dates, I contacted a friend of mine from college, Dan Graybeal, who worked at Cornell University in Ithaca, New York at the time. Dan grew up in Smyth County, Virginia and has numerous relatives/ancestors from the Grayson/Ashe areas, so he "knows" the actual area where these families lived. On 17 October 2005, I received an email from Mr. Graybeal with his assessment of the likelihood of each date/year as the

---

[13] Hash, Hurdle. Social Security Index, jpeg image, (Online: The Generations Network, Inc., 2009) [Digital scan of original records in the National Archives, Washington, DC], subscription database, <http://www.ancestry.com/>, accessed September 2011.

[14] Hash, Hurdle. North Carolina Death Index, 1906-2004, (Online: The Generations Network, Inc., 2009) [Digital scan of original records in the National Archives, Washington, DC], subscription database, <http://www.ancestry.com/>, accessed September 2011.

death date of John and Elizabeth, based solely on weather conditions. Of the two dates, he felt that the weather in early February 1895 was more likely to have wreaked havoc in the mountains where the Hashes lived and consequently died. In the following paragraphs, he describes the likely weather conditions based on data he found in the weather department at Cornell.

"8 February 1895: high and low for the day were +9'F and -7'F, with ~8.5" snowfall preceding over 6--7 Feb -- at Knoxville. These are the only data I have that are as specific as you requested; Knoxville and Asheville are the closest stations 100 yr ago, and Asheville didn't begin until 1902.

"The wind directions at Knoxville indicated the storm moved west, so maybe a ~6 hr delay by the time it reaches Ashe Co. Knowing the elevation difference between K[nox]ville and Ashe Co., it's likely the daily high temperature never got above 0'F in the mountains, on 8 Feb 1895. And, it's likely they got much more than Knoxville's 8" of snow, probably 12"+, maybe even 18--24". Furthermore, the pressures dip pretty low, along with NE winds ahead of the event, indicating a mid-latitude cyclone and the possibility of a good snowstorm."[15]

WHERE DID HE GO?

[15] Email correspondence with Dan Graybeal from17 October 2005.

Regardless of whether John and Elizabeth died in 1892 or 1895, though, I am left with the question of where did John Daniel go immediately following his parents' deaths? With whom did he live? In fact, I had no information on John Daniel from the death of his parents (1892 or 1895) until his marriage to Cora Alberta "Bertie" Davis in Tazewell County, Virginia in 1902. From his parents' death until 1902, his whereabouts and life in general were a mystery to me – until I happened to purchase a re-issued copy of Alleghany County, North Carolina Marriages book in 2007. As I flipped through the pages looking for a totally different family line, I noticed a "John Hash" listed as marrying a "Mary Jane Parish" on 13 March 1897, and laughed, "*Oh, look! Another John Hash!*" I looked at his age, though, and the information listed for the couple being married. This "other" John Hash was listed as being 18 years old – about the age of my John Daniel Hash; and the parents' names listed were "John and Elizabeth."[16] Upon procuring a copy of the marriage license from Alleghany County, I learned that this John Hash's parents John & Elizabeth were dead at the time of his marriage to Mary Jane Parish, as was her father, Henderson Parish. With the commonality of the names John and Elizabeth, especially in that time period, I proceeded with caution, wanting to make sure that I could confirm my suspicions.

---

[16] Latham, George Henry. Alleghany County, North Carolina Marriages 1849-1900. West Minster, MD: Heritage, 1996. Republished 2007.

So I looked on Ancestry.com for the 1900 Alleghany County, North Carolina census for a "John Hash." None were found; a Mary Jane Hash, was discovered, though, and living with her were two small boys, Casper and Chester, born July 1898 and May1900 respectively, and Mary Jane's mother, Susie (Susa) Parish.[17] What I had discovered, again quite unintentionally, was not only where John Daniel Hash was during at least part of the time between his parents' death and 1902, but also an entire family that *my* family had never known about! But where was he in the 1900 census? Why wasn't he with his wife and two small sons? And how had he landed in Tazewell County shortly after that to marry my great-great-grandmother and begin the only family I thought he had? As always seemed to be the case with this man, one question answered seemed to lead to at least two new ones to try to figure out.

My theory on John Daniel's whereabouts during the 1900 census again leads to more speculation and guessing on my part. In McDowell County, West Virginia, a county that borders Tazewell County, Virginia and is part of the "coal fields" of that region has not one, but two, John Hashes listed for that particular census, both listed as

---

[17] 1900 U.S. Federal Census (Population Schedule), Piney Creek Township, Alleghany, North Carolina, Sheet 10, Line 86, Mary Jane Parish household, jpeg image, (Online: The Generations Network, Inc., 2009) [Digital scan of original records in the National Archives, Washington, DC], subscription database, <http://www.ancestry.com/>, accessed September 2011.

"boarders," likely making them workers in coal mines in that area. One is a John Hash, age 22, born in March 1878, single, born in Virginia, father born in Virginia, mother born in Virginia, shown as being a "day laborer [in] Sandy," and a boarder in the household of Columbus Murphy;[18] the second one is a John Hash, age 27, born in April 1873, single, born in Virginia, father born in Virginia, mother born in Virginia, shown as being a "house carpenter" in the Elkhorn district of McDowell County, in the household of James B. Hill.[19] Neither man is listed as married, but if one of them is John Daniel Hash, he may have claimed "single" status to ward off questions from other boarders or nosy landlords. If one of them was indeed John Daniel Hash, maybe he considered himself single because he had left Alleghany County, North Carolina to start a new life. Maybe he had left Alleghany County to find work and decided upon arriving that living and working in this area was more to his liking than being a husband and father. Again, all of these are just potential scenarios. To this point

[18] 1900 U.S. Federal Census (Population Schedule), Sandy, McDowell, West Virginia, Sheet 33, Line 28, Columbus Murphy household, jpeg image, (Online: The Generations Network, Inc., 2009) [Digital scan of original records in the National Archives, Washington, DC], subscription database, <http://www.ancestry.com/>, accessed September 2011.

[19] 1900 U.S. Federal Census (Population Schedule), Elkhorn District, McDowell, West Virginia, Sheet 22, Line 13, James B. Hill household, jpeg image, (Online: The Generations Network, Inc., 2009) [Digital scan of original records in the National Archives, Washington, DC], subscription database, <http://www.ancestry.com/>, accessed September 2011.

in my research, this part of his life has remained shrouded in unknowns.

JOHN DANIEL HASH'S LIFE IN TAZEWELL COUNTY

John Daniel Hash and his second wife, Bertie (my great-great-grandmother) had ten children. Their names and birth years are as follows: Laura Ellen (1870), Noah Ellis (1873), Elizabeth Catharine (1874), John Raleigh (1876), William Clay (1877), Nancie A. (1880), Martha A. (1882), Cora Alberta (1884), Mintie A. (1886), and AJ [male] (1888). The 1910 census lists the first three children – Annie L[ou], Thomas J[ackson], and Leola M[ary];[20] their fourth child, Daisy Irene Hash, was born on 30 July 1910 and therefore is not listed on that census. Once again, John Daniel seems to vanish by the 1920 census, appearing nowhere on the census for Tazewell County, or any county adjoining Tazewell County (either in Virginia, North Carolina, or West Virginia); the entire family, as a matter of fact, shows up on no census for these counties, or for Grayson, Ashe, or Alleghany. Perhaps the census-taker missed them; perhaps they had briefly moved elsewhere but were not still in that place when the census was actually

[20] 1910 U.S. Federal Census (Population Schedule), Jeffersonville District, Tazewell, Virginia, Page 18B, Line 60, John Hash household, jpeg image, (Online: ProQuest Company, 2009) [Digital scan of original records in the National Archives, Washington, DC], subscription database, <http://www.heritagequestonline.com/>, accessed 31 August 2011.

taken. Again, there are no clear answers to the questions raised by the family's "disappearance" from Tazewell County's 1920 census. By 1930, however, they are again on the census for Tazewell County, Virginia and are listed with Walter, age 16; William, age 13; Ruth, 10; Sadie, age 8; Paul, age 6, and John A[llen], age 4.[21] My great-grandmother, their daughter Daisy Irene, had married on 29 November 1926, so she never appeared on a census with her family, not having been born until July 1910 and the family having apparently been missed altogether from a 1920 census. I hope that recording that fact herein will keep someone somewhere at some point in the future from thinking that she did not exist as part of John Daniel and Bertie's brood of children.

On his World War I Draft Card, the following information is given for John Daniel Hash: full name: John Hash (no middle name or initial recorded); permanent home address is North Tazewell (in Tazewell County), Virginia; age is 40 years; date of birth is February 17th 1878; race is white; U.S. citizen, native-born; employed by John D. Peery of North Tazewell, Virginia; nearest relative is given as Bertie Hash of N. Tazewell, Virginia. His height is recorded as "tall," and his build is "medium." His eyes are

[21] 1930 U.S. Federal Census (Population Schedule), Jeffersonville District, Tazewell, Virginia, Page 41A, Line 5, John Hash household, jpeg image, (Online: ProQuest Company, 2009) [Digital scan of original records in the National Archives, Washington, DC], subscription database, <http://www.heritagequestonline.com/>, accessed 31 August 2011.

reportedly [g]rey, and his hair color is "mixed [b]lack and [g]rey." In regards to any lost limbs, eyes, or obvious physical reasons to keep him from service, the word "no" appears on the card.[22] On his World War II Draft Card, much the same information is given – the full name is again recorded as John Hash, this time a line through the area above the space for "middle name," with a permanent address of North Tazewell, Virginia. His age is listed as 61 years and his birthdate is recorded as February 17th 1881, a discrepancy of three years from the information recorded on the World War I Draft Card. Place of birth on the Draft Card for World War II names Grayson County, Virginia as John Daniel's place of birth. For the name and address of the person who would always know his address, John Daniel listed Joe Litz of N. Tazewell, Virginia, the man he also listed as his employer.[23]

---

[22] Hash, John. World War I Draft Cards, jpeg image, (Online: The Generations Network, Inc., 2009) [Digital scan of original records in the National Archives, Washington, DC], subscription database, <http://www.ancestry.com/>, accessed September 2011.

[23] Hash, John. World War II Draft Cards, jpeg image, (Online: The Generations Network, Inc., 2009) [Digital scan of original records in the National Archives, Washington, DC], subscription database, <http://www.ancestry.com/>, accessed September 2011.

[24] Marriage license and certificate for John Hash and Lula Marson [Morrison], Tazewell County Clerk's Office, Tazewell, Virginia.

Bertie Davis Hash died in the spring of 1932. On 31 October 1936, in Tazewell County, Virginia, John Daniel Hash married again, this time to Lula Warden "Marson" (correctly spelled "Morrison"), also widowed and living in North Tazewell, Virginia.[24] The couple had no children and remained together until John Daniel's death in 1955. John and Bertie are reportedly buried next to each other in a Peery family cemetery on Fairgrounds Road in Tazewell. Their graves are unmarked, however, and only known to one of their living grandchildren. Even the final resting place of John Daniel Hash has left me with more questions than answers, but they are questions for which I continue to seek answers.

Poetry: Lyrics and Verse

(Photo of Chrissie Anderson and Melenia Edwards, circa 1986-1987'ish, Castlewood, VA)

Warning: Message From a 16-Year-Old Me

Don't push me now,
for I may fall;
I'm not quite as stable
as you think.

One careless word
could easily crush me,
for I'm standing
on the brink.

Don't think I'm overreacting –
I'm serious,
dead serious
(not suicidal).

I'm emotional;
I'm human;
you see, I am fragile;
handle with care.

If you'll only speak softly,
not loudly, uncaring.
I'm tired of people
telling me what to do.

I'm me – I'm a teenager.
I can only do so much.
I'm not perfect,
please accept me.

Don't tell me I'm some dummy.
Don't tell me I'm not your child.
Just hold me;
I'm crying.

People think I'm happy.
I don't tell them otherwise.
They expect it –
I can't let them down.

Sometimes it seems I'm trapped
in the shadows of myself,
the "fake" me –
not the one found deep inside.
I'm sixteen and I'm a person.
I only need some love.
Please don't push me –
I may crumble.

Sometimes, I watch my candle
as it flickers in the wind
and I see myself
struggling to continue living.

Then the light goes out
and I'm crying again,
'cos I don't want to die;
I've just begun to live.

So I reach out
and hold on tightly
'til the next time –

watching out,
hoping dearly
that someone will help me up
so I won't tumble
and crash loudly.

Please don't push me,
for I'm not stable
and I may fall down
like the rain does:

Crashing thunder,
brilliant sunlight,
dreary cloudbursts,
hazy moonlight,
stormy weather,
cold wind blowing,
rivers surging,
dainty snowflakes.

Hear my calling,
gentle sobbing;
just don't push me:
this is a warning.

I Cried

I cried for you
last night;
I cried
for what
never was,
what might
have been;
in the end,
I cried
for nothing.

(Photo by Sarah Swartzendruber Shaffer, Seattle, WA)

We tend to write best about cultures that have almost melted into the past. The blue valleys, the fog-haunted coves, the tireless milky waterfalls, are still there, but the people, the people with wisdom in their hands and humility in their hearts, have slipped away forever, unless we find them in our own words, and in our own hands and hearts.
– Robert Morgan

Mountaintops in Memories

Oh, mountaintops in memories:

I call to mind
your colors,
the dazzling wonderment
of your landscape,
of plumaged fowl
and fur-covered brethren,
of ridges that met the sky,
smoky blues melting
into slate-hued heavens;
now slate has given way
mere darkness.

I will to life again

your woodlands,
mighty oaks, splendid cedars,
even chestnut trees of old,
all thriving on your hillsides
on sacred yesterdays.
How tall you grew, how proud
before we ripped you down,
and trucked you out for profit.

I close my eyes to recapture
places held in high regard,
high esteem by all of nature,
high cliff lines strung way up;
your precipices, refuge for people
treated like animals too long,
protected like precious treasures,
that red-skinned Eastern Band,
while others marched sadly West.

I see again in your dawn-fog
all those who once lived here:
creatures crafting homes
from your timbers, who
wove tight and secure
your sacred grasses,
marked passages of time
on your creek banks,

until all of those were gone.

I try not to remember
the people, those who scarred
your heart, dug deep to harvest
your lungs, ripped off your
beautiful timber-lined skin,
corroded your bloodlines with
chemical run-off, made a
mockery of your children
and blew the hell out of all you afforded.

(Photo courtesy of LEAF and Patricia Hudson;
Zeb Mountain in Campbell County, TN;
http://tnleaf.org/legislative/links-for-legislation/photos)

In the Spirit

She danced in the spirit,
round-round, round-round
the little church
on the hillside,
in the middle of the curve
as you drive towards
Baptist Valley.
Hands raised in holy hosannas,
down-down, down-down
the fiery tongues descended
before the altar
where she shouted
words only hearts
could comprehend.
Convulsing in lovely arches,
keeping time, keeping time
shoes slipped out of
and red skirt fanning
the Holy Ghost atop her,
within her
rhythmic writhing.
Sweat sparkling on her forehead,
slowing, slowing
like a carousel ride
ending calmly —

the bobbing pole abating
and her body slumping, slain
in the spirit, at peace.

(Photo by Chrissie Anderson Peters)

Gina and Tommy, Revisited: 2013

"Gina works the diner all day,
Working for her man, she brings home her pay
For love – for love…
Gina dreams of running away,
When she cries in the night, Tommy whispers, 'It's
okay…'" – from "Living on a Prayer" by Bon Jovi

Who didn't know their story?
Late-80's teenaged couple
giving love all they had:
living on a prayer, living in sin,
victims of the striking union on
the docks, believers of the dream
that love could see them through,
if only they tried.

But really – who wanted to be Gina?
A worn-out, teenage girl,
exhausted from manual labor
in a low-class sleazy diner,
with greasy-haired guys
making passes, touching
hair, hips, boobs, and butt –
but never her heart or mind.

Tripping on broken promises
and well-intentioned lyrics,

romantic riffs her man used
to play before he lost even his
six-string, that last remainder –
lone reminder – of life
before she ran away to show
them all she'd make it just fine.

No, Tommy – it's *not* okay!
She should've stayed in school,
should've gone to college, found
a guy with a good degree and
a steady job, someone who
would ask if he could marry her,
and someday maybe take her
to a Bon Jovi concert.

(Photo, Chrissie Anderson Peters, Bon Jovi Concert, Charlotte, NC, March 2013)

Lifetime

(Lyrics, Song for Mamaw & Papaw Little's
50th Wedding Anniversary, 1998)

A lifetime of living,
a lifetime of love,
a lifetime surviving
when push comes to shove;
a lifetime of moments
the two of you share,
a lifetime believing
you'll always be there.

(Chorus)
In a lifetime, two people meet;
in a lifetime, make each other complete;
in a lifetime that goes through the years
a lifetime of smiling through tears.

A lifetime of troubles,
a lifetime of hope,
a lifetime of dreaming,
but learning to cope;
a lifetime of struggles,
but seeing it through,
a lifetime of giving
always comes back to you.

(Chorus)
In a lifetime, two people meet;
in a lifetime, make each other complete;
in a lifetime that goes through the years
a lifetime of smiling through tears.

It's your lifetime,
just keep holding hands;
it's your lifetime
where you've learned to understand;
it's your lifetime –
what else could you do?
Just hold onto forever
and make it come true.

Lifetime.

(Family photo of Arthur James Little & Dorothy Irene Vance Little on their wedding day, 2 July 1948, Tazewell, VA)

Hibernation

Autumn's chill
comes marching
like a seasoned soldier
steeling my heartbeat,
    stealing my heartbeat,
        stilling my heartbeat
        again.

(Photo by Chrissie Anderson Peters,
somewhere on the WV Turnpike, Summer 2013)

In Season

Rifle shots echo
across ridges
down hollers
through valleys
off hillsides.
Men and mere boys
honing their skills,
more instinct than ingenuity,
practicing,
perfecting
an age-old craft
a primal rite of passage,
conditioning for the kill,
dreaming of the drama,
envisioning their sites
on the prize.
Meanwhile
an 8-point buck
and docile-eyed doe
perk their ears,
point their noses,
in the relative safety
of my backyard.

October Evening, Grayson County

Blowing down backroads like
October breezes shaking Summer
from sumacs, ushering Autumn
right in; the sun setting on
rugged ridges, jagged jawlines
of mountains, bare bottoms by
creek beds reflecting again.

Cow paths climb, careful, winding
their way home, 'round hillsides,
through hollers, over age-old
oak trees. Stone chimneys bear
witness to way-gone remembrances,
from so-long sojourners
who'll pass by here no more.

Just leave those reminders, those
ram-rod remainders, just give me
tomorrows tinged with yesterday's
news; give me the memories, the
hoped-for someday-soons; hold
hands in the moonlight
once more before dawn.

Blow Me Home

Oh, salty South Carolina winds
wet with mist and memories
blow me home through coastal sands,
past North Carolina's Piedmont paths,
through Virginia valleys below blue ridges.
Blow me back to that Tennessee town
where mountains wait to embrace me.

("Morning Blues," Photo by Pat Shrader, Blue Ridge
Expressions, B&W version for book only)

Mary, Holding Court

On the occasion of
her 95th birthday,
dressed in bonnie
baby blue, seated
serenely on her scooter,
a semi-circle of women
surround her, talking,
laughing, remembering
people, places, and events
from mileposts of life;
they listen intently
as she tells a story,
proffers some explanation,
recalls some glory from
bygone days,
blue eyes bubbling
with energy, excitement,
enthusiasm – with
every good thing
that a lifetime can hold;
and time stands still
for a moment,
with a mid-May
breeze blowing,
love bugs lingering,

and the Florida
humidity held
humbly at bay:
and I smile at this
woman, her amazing
beauty, impeccable
posture, perfectly
lined and colored
lips as she surveys
those around her, those
come to honor her,
to celebrate her
lifetime, to lift up
their own monarch
in her prime.

(Photo by Chrissie Anderson Peters, of Mary Palmer Gathman, the weekend of Mary's 95th birthday, Ft. McCoy, FL)

Please Don't Make Me Color

Please don't make me color!
I will sit here and write
letters for you all day
long. I will read about Bing
and Sandy – out loud if you
want me to. I'll even sit beside
stinky Linda G., even though she
scares me, just please don't make
me color!

I'll let some other lucky
girl sit beside Stevie Gallagher
and some other girl can
share her lunch with that
cutie Chris Whittaker. I'll
write on the blackboard, spell
big words out loud, or even take
the lunch count over to Ms. Asbury
in the cafeteria in the rain, but
please don't make me color!

Don't make me draw anything –
not people, not animals, not
houses, not cars. Last year, in
kindergarten, all the kids

made fun of my pictures; they
can't see them like I see
them, so I must see them wrong.
I know for sure I color them
wrong, Miss Brown and Miss Sluss
told me so – people and cows
are not purple; the sky is blue,
not orange; and nobody
in Tazewell lives in a house with
stripes, no matter how pretty
the colors are to me.

No, please, don't make me
Color. You can stick me
between Yolanda and Freddie
and I'll keep her from taking
his pencils and hiding them
and that means that he won't
cry; but please, don't make
me color.

Pathways
(Lyrics)

A hundred thoughts
were racing through my mind
as I traveled down so many paths
I thought I'd never find
and I wondered why I
wandered down this road
I guess there were so many answers
that I thought I had to know.
But the answers turned
to questions in a dream
and I learned that no solution
is ever as it seems,
so I smiled and shrugged my shoulders,
set to leave,
'cos there are countless other
pathways left to see.
Each and every day
a new world is at hand
with a crowd of crazy puzzles
we may never understand,
but we do the best
with what we have to do,
maybe what is right for me
will never be quite right for you.

still we press along
to unseen distant goals
and we draw our strength from somewhere
else, like two magnetic poles
and we try to bring some peace
into the fight
as we smile ourselves to sleep
this silent night.

(Photo by Chrissie Anderson Peters, Faerie Glen, Isle of Skye, Scotland, with permission from the faeries)

Poets Under the Skin

Square pegs
forced into round holes,
no matter how hard we try;
we see the world
in different hues,
colors that don't exist
inside any Crayola box;
we hear its songs
in different harmonies,
in keys that complement
without intention
or deliberation;
we feel with emotions
set to a different frequency,
like bats with sonar
we fly by day,
soar to heights unmeasured,
dive to lows unimagined
by common cardinals and crows,
all because
we are poets
under the skin.

Late November Sky

Steel-silver clouds
stack up like the
blue-hazed mountains
rising below them,
earth and sky brushed
together with only naked
trees to distinguish
where each blends
into the other.

Slate-gray skies
slide across the horizon,
leaking promises like candy
from a ruptured piñata;
creek-beds surge
like swollen bellies
of women whose
womb-fruit hangs low,
past time for their labor.

Foreclosure

The sign outside tells a story,
not the whole truth,
but a story:
paints a picture
of irresponsibility;
sends a signal
of fiscal negligence,
never mind whatever
reasons might exist
for such a fate
to befall us.
It is definitively
our American dream
deferred, deflated, and forgone:
a dream that might as well
be forgotten.
A modern-day scarlet letter:
this time, an F,
a glowering, towering F,
announcing: "We floundered!"
"We fumbled!"
"We effed-
up our future!"
Never mind
that we were forced to fold,

after falling flat.
What matters is that
the world sees us
in all our
abject failure,
surmises our fall
from grace,
feeds on our frustration
and foundering,
our frankly un-finessed finale:
Foreclosure.

(Photo by Chrissie Anderson Peters, Ashe County, NC)

Running From Crazy

"I've been running from
crazy my whole life." I
laugh; I make it sound
light-hearted, make it sound
like a joke, make it sound
like a Southern saying, wrap
my lips around it in a smile,
and kiss it softly, trying not to
choke on its repulsiveness,
trying not to catch myself on
its ragged edges, trying harder
not to get pulled into the
delusions or mirages that play
havoc with the minds of my
kinfolks, my family, the
ancestors who have died in the
state mental facility, or who
should have died there for all the
good "coming home" ever did them;
trying not to look too deeply into
the eyes of one whose electro-shock-
therapy took more than mere
memories and left much less
than a person. I choke back my
nightmares, salted with childhood

crying, with teenage entanglements,
and out-and-out adult angst, take
another long gulp of bittersweet
reality, and force a smile as I
tell you again, "Yes-sir-ee, I've
been running from crazy
my whole life…"

(Drawing by Kacper Lengiewicz, London, England)

Tonight She Sleeps Alone

Tonight she sleeps alone with thoughts and dreams
Heavy beats the heart within its chamber
Not ev'rything is always as it seems
Amidst her rest hidden there lies danger.

His honeyed tongue did dally with her head
His jade eyes too long upon her lingered
His heart betrayed her in that same bless'd bed
Whereupon her lacy fringe he fingered.

And held her in his arms til midnight struck
His lips pressed firm upon her heaving breasts
Then plunged a dagger deep til fast it stuck
A pool of rose formed thick upon her chest.

Now pumping out the life that sure is death
The maiden sleeps alone, all out of breath.

Her

Her long blonde hair sways, always alluring because
I never have the patience to let mine grow.
Maybe it's magic to run fingers through such fineness,
to inhale its freshness up close. I've wanted to start
brushing from crown downward, toward her shoes,
soft satin like creamy ballet slippers, the same
pallor as facial paleness kissed by dew.
Perhaps some august accident could make her see me,
in my passionate imperfections, help her
to know the secrets stored inside me, songs and surety.
"Go on," I want to tell her. "Make those necessary
changes to be with me, let your long hair tangle us
like honeysuckle. Sting like static cling. Wrap me up safe.
You are the dream I never knew I needed to come true."

(Photo by Chrissie Anderson Peters, Fleetwood Mac Concert, Louisville, KY, April 2013)

Unable to Swim

I'm being dragged to the edge
kicking and screaming again.
Over and over, through tall grass
that slashes at my ankles and wrists,
and pulled through the mud
where my feet dig in, seeking
toeholds, handholds, anything,
some way to keep from going under.

"Dear God." I am screaming,
some primal voice, deep and foreign;
am I praying, or merely calling
out to anyone for help, out to
any force or deity, as if any
can exist here, as if anyone can hear,
as if anything can help, as if any
help exists outside the prison of my mind?

The murky water creeps around me,
static singing from the past
humming in my eardrums as my head
goes under, my eyes wide open, seeing
nothing, and more than nothing, less
than nothing, yet ever-nothing; brown
creek oozing its desolation over and around
me, in and out my orifices, bubbling up.

Drowning out my screaming,
obliterating my tears,
choking down last night's dinner
as it tries to make its way out;
invisible hands holding me,
touching me, taunting me,
threatening me not to try to float;
reminding me that I can't swim.

(Photo of Neist Point in Isle of Skye, Scotland, by Chrissie Anderson Peters, editing assistance by Pat Shrader)

(The Memories of) The Lonely Crowd
(Song Lyrics)

(Chorus)
Past is past and now is now,
The memories of the lonely crowd;
The tears they cried, the joy inside,
The memories of the lonely crowd.

Oh, the pain that is their mind,
They fear not let it show today,
The memories of the lonely crowd are made.
Oh, their lies were told unto the world,
And passion spoke aloud
Pride destroyed throughout the lonely crowd.

(Chorus)
Past is past and now is now,
The memories of the lonely crowd;
The tears they cried, the joy inside,
The memories of the lonely crowd.

For the love of one who would not come,
It all was thrown away,
Never to return unto this day.
Oh, the voices speak inside their heads,
The music makes a rhyme,

And the lonely crowd repays the crime.

(Chorus)
Past is past and now is now,
The memories of the lonely crowd;
The tears they cried, the joy inside,
The memories of the lonely crowd.

The love of all that let it fall,
The memories of the lonely crowd;
The taste of fate that made them wait,
The memories of the lonely crowd.

(Photo by Chrissie Anderson Peters, North Tazewell
Elementary School Playground, N. Tazewell, VA,
23 October 2013)

Woodpecker

For years he has disrupted all my work:
Wherever in the house I choose to write
Outside some windowsill he seems to lurk
I scream and curse until he takes to flight.

But then he comes again to agitate,
To break my concentration once again!
Pecking, pecking, never shall he abate,
Drilling on with his bill on wood and tin.

Then one day, behold a glorious sight!
He sits upon the porch rail, still as stone.
A big fat yellow tom cat there alights
And now that damned ol' woodpecker is gone!

May peace and quiet reign throughout the house;
Too bad for him ol' Tom spied not a mouse!

A New Day Dawned

A new day dawned.
Not bright and cheerful,
but with rain and darkness
that echoed my heart.
Regardless of how it
arrived, a new day presented
itself nonetheless.
My losses just a little bump
in the universal grind,
reminding me that it was
fine to slow down a little,
to take time to recuperate,
to pull myself together
in order to begin to heal.
But that the world around me –
and therefore, my place within
it – must also continue
moving forward.

("Blue Ridge Rays," photo by Pat Shrader, B&W version for book only)

About the Author:

(Photo above of Chrissie and Bullmastiff Zeke, and author photo on back cover by Sahara Sparks Photography, Kingsport, TN)

Born and raised in Southwestern Virginia, Chrissie Anderson Peters received stories from those around her from a young age. Many of those stories serve as the frames or foundations of what she writes today.

A 1989 graduate of Tazewell High School, she received her BA from Emory & Henry College (1993) and her Masters of Science in Information Sciences from the University of Tennessee (2002).

Always an avid reader, Chrissie began writing in fourth grade. After college she continued collecting writing ideas, although she did not write much for several years. Her dedication to writing rekindled in 2005 when she took a Creative Writing course at Northeast State Community College, where she worked as a librarian. Since then, her work has been published in *Echoes & Images, Clinch Mountain Review, Pine Mountain Sand & Gravel, The Howl,* and in the acclaimed online publication *Still: The Journal.* She has received accolades in several contests, as well as being accepted at the Hindman Settlement School's Appalachian Writers Workshop (2010-2013). She currently serves as President of the Poetry Society of Tennessee's Northeast Chapter and is also a member of the Appalachian Authors Guild, Boone Tree Library Association, Tennessee Library Association, Tazewell County Historical

Society, and Grayson County (Virginia) Heritage Foundation (of which she is a Board Member).

In addition to writing, Chrissie loves to travel and meet people; she loves getting to know places and people, and their stories. She returned to the US at the end of Summer 2013 from a four-week jaunt through the UK and parts of Europe, a trip that will serve as the backdrop for her third book, *Chasing After Rainbows*, a collection of essays: part travelogue, part planning guide, part adventure tale, part cultural frustration, part social commentary, and part Duran-Duran-fan dream-come-true.

Chrissie and her husband Russ reside in Bristol, Tennessee, with their feline children. *Dog Days and Dragonflies* is her first full-length publication; *Running From Crazy* is her second collection of stories/essays/poems. For more information, check out her website, www.CAPWrites.com, or email her at TheWriteWayToGo@gmail.com. Chrissie is available to speak on a variety of topics, ranging from writing to self-publishing and beyond.

About the Book's Cover Artist:

Pat Shrader, owner of Blue Ridge Expressions, is a photographer based in the Asheville/Hendersonville, North Carolina area. His photographs have won multiple awards and reflect the beauty and majesty of the Appalachian Mountains and its people. As a fellow classmate of Chrissie's at both Tazewell High and Emory & Henry College, Pat is excited to be a part of her project based in part on the area that he, too, calls home. Pat, his wife, Heather, and their three beautiful children enjoy the wonderful Blue Ridge Mountains and a tall glass of Sweet Iced Tea. You can view his work at www.BlueRidgeExpressions.com, or follow him on Twitter @BlueRidgePat.

Acknowledgements

We have all heard and can agree that "it takes a village" to raise a child; likewise, it takes far more than an author to bring a book to life. This is the part of a book that always makes me nervous. What if I leave out someone? What if someone gets upset for including him/her by name? Let me just apologize in advance if I leave out anyone or if I call unwanted attention to anyone who has been a positive influence to me over the years. Some people say, "I was only doing my job," or "I don't deserve to be singled out." Obviously, I feel otherwise if I do so!

I have been blessed beyond measure in more ways than I can count. God has opened doors for me in life that I would never have even dreamed of existing, much less of being opened to me at some point in my earlier life. There are days when I literally feel like I have been given more than one life to live, like one person cannot plausibly have been given so many opportunities. Sometimes I have to close my eyes to tears to try to keep it all in focus. That's no exaggeration. I've heard people say that one cannot write "nonfiction" forever, that eventually, one would run out of things to write about. I'm not sure this is true, though, based on what I have lived thus far in my thirteen years of being twenty-nine. I feel like I could write forever about what has happened to me and the people I know. Sometimes I "doctor it up with fiction," though, because I am Murphy's Law Incarnate and bizarre-o things happen to me that most people would find difficult to believe were true. (For example, only one detail in "Diner Dude" did not happen in that diner in Chattanooga; I leave for the reader to figure out which or to come to one of my programs and ask about it.) Having said that, though, I do sometimes write other people's stories, so, just because I have written it doesn't mean that it is necessarily about my life/me. I'm an honest liar. Smiles.

I've been fortunate enough to have some of the most amazing educators to grace the mountains of Virginia and Tennessee. To each of you, I say thank you. And to those who continue to do so today, long after the classrooms stand behind us (like Susan Whittaker and Nancy Wallace from Tazewell High School, who continuously lift me up on support me on Facebook; and Dr. Bill Robinson from the University of Tennessee, who never rejects my requests to serve as a judge for the book cover contest and always gives great guidance and judicial wisdom for me to consider, as well), I not only say "thank you," but also offer my heartfelt love; you have no idea how much you three, especially, mean to me!

For this particular project, I wish to thank Rita Sims Quillen and Rebecca Elswick, who both made time to read and provide author blurbs for this project when many others could not. Your friendship, both professional and personal, both humbles me and illustrates what the writing community should be about. So again, I bow deep in gratitude to you both!

Thanks not only to Dr. Bill Robinson, but to my other book cover judges on the *Running From Crazy* project: Ann Clapp (Nolensville, TN); Jay McCoy (Louisville, KY); and Keith Stewart (Hyden, KY). I believe that your choice was a great one and look forward to touting its image along with my words for a long time to come.

In choosing Pat Shrader's book cover for *Running From Crazy*, that committee gave me not only a marvelous book cover for this collection, but also a rekindling of friendship that has brought a unique partnership to the project. Without Pat's perspective, I'd be rather lost on a number of points. He changed color pictures to black and white for me, cropped me out of pictures I didn't need to be in.

All without complaint. He read over the manuscript and gave his opinion on the order of things. He also listened to me go on and on about my trip to the UK/Europe and helped me come to the decision about a title for the book that will result from those grand adventures. His input has been invaluable and appreciated more than I can express! For these things and so many more, thanks, Pat!

To Virginia Salmon, Matthew Whitenack Kingesly, and Tasha Neel Hicks for reading the entire manuscript for me, and to Virginia for her tireless efforts in editing the manuscript. Again, any mistakes you find herein are likely my fault, not hers whatsoever!

To everyone who has given me a chance to speak or to sell my work at your venues/events in the past nearly 18 months, I am grateful beyond words. Especially since I left my full-time library job at the end of January 2013, these opportunities are so important to me! This is where I know I will leave out folks, so please forgive me if I do. From Hindman Settlement School allowing us to set out books during the Appalachian Writers Workshop and Lincoln Memorial University permitting us to do the same on Saturday night's festivities during the Mountain Heritage Literary Festival; to my amazing friend Vickie Combs, who pulled strings, bent rules, and blazed a path I didn't think was possible in order to see me have a "proper" book launch at Barnes & Noble in Johnson City, TN, I owe you more than I can ever repay; there may not be a character specifically based on you in the pages of *RFC*, but your character is all over it, my friend! To the fine folks involved with the following organizations/venues, where I have spoken/signed, huge thanks, as well: Pine Mountain Sand & Gravel; Boone Tree Library Association; Kristy Robinson Horine with the Licking Valley Writers Workshop; Frontier Christmas at Historic Crab Orchard (special thanks to Charlotte G. Whitted); Tazewell County Historical Society; Main Street Moments;

Appalachian Arts Center (Richlands, VA); Grayson County Virginia Heritage Foundation; Bluefield College's Appalachian Festival; Poetry Society of Tennessee, Northeast Chapter; Night Writers Guild (Tri-Cities, TN); Tennessee Library Association; Northeast State Community College; Back of the Dragon Festival (Tazewell, VA); Graham Middle School (Bluefield, VA); North Tazewell Elementary School (North Tazewell, VA); Jeanne Powers at Bristol Public Library; and Joe Tennis and Sharon Mishler Fox (*Bristol Herald Courier*), Jim Talbert (*Clinch Valley News* and *Richlands News Press*), and Bill Archer (*Bluefield Daily Telegraph*), for featuring me in write-ups in local papers; as well as others I know I am missing.

To each person who has purchased a copy of any of my work – electronically or in paperback – or who has accepted a copy as a gift from me for some personal or professional kindness, another thank you. To each person who has kindly mentioned my name or my work to others, another debt of gratitude. My readers are my best PR, so I appreciate you especially! Also in this category, super-special kudos go to John Rhudy and his family in Burke's Garden. John, his son Ian, his daughter Abigail, and his wife Bethany, talked up my first book and looked for speaking and selling opportunities for me when it seemed like no one else in Tazewell was interested in my work at all. Ian and Abigail have handed out flyers and bookmarks at events; John and Bethany told friends and neighbors about my work. It means a lot when people are willing to do that.

To each place that has agreed to take copies of my work and try to sell them, sometimes for a small commission for the owner/manager, sometimes for a small percentage donated to a good cause, and sometimes just because you love me and believe in my work, I appreciate your willingness to try to help. These places include Barnes & Noble (Johnson City, TN); Clip N Curl (Tazewell, VA, thanks, Janice!); Shoney's (Exit 5, Bristol, VA, special thanks to Brian & Susan Spencer); Appalachian Arts Center (Richlands, VA); City Lights Bookstore (Sylva, NC); The Wild Fig (Lexington, KY); Morris Book Shop (Lexington, KY); and the Mercantile Bookstore at Emory & Henry College (Emory, VA). I hope that all of you will be willing to stock *Running From Crazy*, as well!

I never want to forget to thank my family. Without them, I wouldn't be who I am. (Now you know who to blame it on! Just kidding!) They might not always understand who I am or why I am the way I am, but they love me. And I love them. That's what family is supposed to do. I hope that they understand why I've written this book and that it's about my own struggles, ultimately, and not about familial shortcomings or anything that they might perceive to be that way.

To Matthew Whitenack Kingesly, my webmaster and PR guru, I could write pages and pages of thanks just to you. Thank you for making me look good, sound smart, and stay more on top of things. You certainly have your hands full, but I am exceptionally glad that you took me on as a client, as well as keeping me as your friend for all these long years.

To Shian Sparks, my amazed gratitude for a new set of remarkable "author pics" from this past Spring. Several friends/readers participated in a panel to help select the "official" photos that would be used for the book (the one that appears on page 147, as well as the back cover). It was a really tough decision, so I was glad for the assistance! I can't begin to thank everyone who helped by name – so please just know that I love you and appreciate you taking the time to look through the pictures and rank your favorites!

I wish to thank my husband, Russ, not only for loving me and for putting up with the quirkiness that writers are so well known for, but also for giving me every opportunity in the world to fly, both figuratively and literally! In the same calendar year, you allowed me to quit my library job (drastically cutting our income) to pursue writing "fuller" time, and allowed me to spend money that we didn't necessarily have to take off to the UK and Europe, *Chasing After Rainbows* (which will be the name of the book resulting from that trip), starting with a 29-year-long dream of meeting John Taylor, bassist extraordinaire of Duran Duran, in Edinburgh, Scotland, for what may have been the last of the book events for his autobiography, *In the Pleasure Groove.* I had no idea when planning the trip what else lay in store across the ocean, but to call it the most amazing 28 days of my life thus far is truly an understatement! (After all, in addition to John Taylor, I met author Margaret Atwood, Neil Gaiman for a second time in the same Summer, Dom Brown – current lead guitarist for Duran Duran, the Maasai Cricket Warriors from Kenya, and some Indian singers who I never quite got the names of. That's not too shabby for 28 days!) I shared that time with so many interesting people – I made friends all over the UK, in France, in Italy – and was scared witless by one customs official upon reentry to the UK after leaving Rome. And Russ allowed me to do most of that on my own (well, with my friend Tasha Neel Hicks), as came home after ten days, not standing guard over me. I guess because he knew that I'd come out of it all alive and enlightened. Or at least, more experienced and ready to write it all down. And I am. Now that *Running From Crazy* is finished, my attention will turn to *Chasing After Rainbows* and those magnificent adventures/misadventures; and those friends of mine, new and already acquainted, who still make me miss it all every day and look for any little reason to get back over there to revisit these places, but especially these fine people.

Along those lines, I want to thank an online community of people who have come to mean a great deal to me in the past six months or so, too. I went to Twitter not to find a new group of people to hang out with online, but to learn more about marketing my writing. And I went unhappily. If you know me at all, you know that *I am not a 140-character character*! I'm still not tremendous at Twitter and admittedly still prefer Facebook as a social media platform. But without Twitter, I wouldn't have met so many phenomenal people who helped encourage and inspire me to finish this collection on days when I thought I couldn't go on. Other writers and thinkers with words of wisdom. But most of all, words of love and light from my Duranie buddies. You know who you are. I can't possibly name all of you, but have to thank Antonella and Sal in Rome for taking in Tasha and me and treating us better than family during our trip, and Priscilla and Julia, for leading me on such exquisite London adventures, like only Duranies could! And I hope that all of my Duranie friends know the incredibly special place that each of you has in my heart!

And then there are the people who have been my friends forever. Or at least for more years than I like to think about. (Kinda like that number I threw out when talking about how long I'd wanted to meet John Taylor – only bigger!) Most of you have known me at my weirdest, my flakiest, my geekiest, and my most unsure moments in life; but you've also known me at my most vulnerable, most heartfelt, and most humanly sincere times. (Maybe you've even been beside me at those moments when I felt like I'd managed to get away from crazy, which we all knew was a delusion of grandeur.) A very special group of you have been there through all of that with me and I couldn't be prouder to call you my friends. *We* are *the Lonely Crowd*, forever, in my mind.

CAP

SPECIAL KICKSTARTER RECOGNITION

Near the end of the writing of the *Running From Crazy* project, I was presented with a special opportunity by the owner of Nubivagant Records (@NubivagantMusic on Twitter and on Facebook at https://www.facebook.com/NubivagantRecords), an indie recording company. I had been knocking around the idea of doing an audio version of a book, especially after being told by friends/ readers in the UK and Australia that they loved my accent and would love to hear me read an entire book. This, after some of them heard an interview done by my dear and incredibly supportive friend, "**Marie Direction**," for her radio show (aptly named "Keep Hearing Voices") in Louisville, KY. Marie, I'm thanking you in this section of the book for several reasons, but primarily, because I credit *you* with beginning my international sales. And I want to go on record as saying that **Catherine Jensen** in Australia was the first person to really encourage me to do an audio version of my work.

With the help of friends/associates from literally all over the world, we raised $1356 through a Kickstarter project and another $185 in donations towards materials and other things for the project. I was completely overwhelmed by the generosity of so many wonderful people! Here is the list of donors for the audio book project:

Diana Anderson; Karen Anderson; Anonymous; Leanne Scalf Barbour; Jenny Poston Bishop; Lynne Bishop; Karen Booth (karenbooth.net); Sharee Bowman; Shelby Brown; Rebecca Baldwin Cisco; Myrica Cook; Glenna Cordill (England); Dee Crescitelli; Diana Cruz (Brazil); Tamara Davis; Stephanie Day; Donna Fifer; Jennifer Fishel; Nancy Flowe; Marilee Glover; Dan Greene; A. Diane Hamilton (www.adianehamilton.com); Kandace Kiser Howlett; Catherine Jensen (Australia); John

Lane; Barbara Cosner Little; Elaine Drennon Little; Erick Long; Denton Loving; Anna Buchanan Martin; Anthony Maxwell; Lenora L. McCloud; Tanzi Merritt; Ian, Lynda, & Tommy Mortimer (New Zealand); Karen Burleson Nave; Reva Pruett; Jennifer Frye Reed; Dina Rice; Kerry Robinson; Jeanette Moore Rogers; Benjamin Russ; Staci Schoenfeld; Mira Selm; Sarah Shaffer; Charlotte Singleton-Abshire; Aaron Smith; Belinda Smith; Keith Stewart; Christi Copeland Stapleton; Francine Marie Tognotti (Frannie Rhodes/ PrudenceBlak); Lesley Tsourdalakis (Australia); Linda Van Dyke; Scotty Vanhoozier; Carole Waters; Chris White; Lesley W. (Scotland); Sherrie Wicker; and Maja Z. (Australia).

I can't help but shed some tears of happiness alongside the smile on my face when I look over that list! When I think of how many facets of my life each of those names represents, when I consider what amazing gifts your donations are indeed... That is powerful stuff! And, yet again, my dreams have come true in bigger ways than I ever dared to imagine them! When I consider how many of you were not even a part of my life a year ago, I realize even more fully how crazy-cool this great big world we live in is! I love you guys so much! Let's record this book! Let's go, TEAM RUNNING-FROM-CRAZY! (Pompoms have been requested from Santa Claus, Aussie friends!)

Chrissie Anderson Peters

5593588R00096

Made in the USA
San Bernardino, CA
13 November 2013